MW01679766

Life Helping Life

Unleash Your Mind/Body Potential with Essential Oils

Every effort has been made to ensure that the information contained in this book is complete and accurate. However, neither the publisher nor the author is engaged in rendering professional advice or services to the individual reader. The ideas, procedures, and suggestions contained in this book are not intended as a substitute for consulting with your physician and obtaining medical supervision as to any activity, procedure, or suggestion that might affect your health. Accordingly, individual readers must assume responsibility for their own actions, safety, and health, and neither the author nor the publisher shall be liable or responsible for any loss, injury, or damage allegedly arising from any information or suggestion in this book.

All readers are urged to consult with a physician before accepting any of the treatments described in this book or undertaking any form of self-treatment. The publisher does not warrant that a treatment or remedy will unfailingly and uniformly perform as described. Likewise, the publisher does not guarantee that every possible hazard, adverse effect contraindication, precaution, or consequence of overdose is included in the material presented here. The publisher has performed no independent verification of the data reported herein, and expressly disclaims responsibility for any error. All information is represented without guarantees by the authors and publisher, who disclaim all liability in connection with its use.

Essentia Publishing., PO Box 50525, Provo, Utah 84605.

ISBN 0-9675661-0-X

Life Helping Life

Unleash Your Mind/Body Potential with Essential Oils

By Daniel Pénoël, MD
and
Rose-Marie Pénoël

Essentia

Table of Contents

Preface

The publication of "*Life Helping Life*" is very symbolic of a turning point in my career and in the worldwide mission that I with my wife Rose-Marie have been pursuing.

For more than twenty years, I have worked in the field of medical aromatherapy. My work has been intense in many areas: treating patients, doing clinical research, visiting growers and distillers in many countries, writing, giving lectures and seminars. All these activities are our attempts to contribute to the advancement and use of essential oils at many levels—from highly specialized medical care to general medicine, from naturopathic care to basic use inside the family, from aromatic care in acute and severe medical conditions to 'wellbeing and harmony' applications.

I have been invited by many firms and companies, by many institutes and organizations, to teach and train the concepts of French medical aromatherapy, embodied in what I call Integrated Aromatic Medicine. I understand that, for an average North American reader, the idea of an MD turning to "aromatherapy" to treat his patients may be a source of astonishment or even shock.

In order to understand why and how I as an MD am seriously and enthusiastically involved in this field, it is important for you to understand that aromatherapy has a much different meaning in France than it does in North America. Essential oils are a major part of our medical system, and are dispensed by pharmacies all over France. In France, aromatherapy is viewed as a legitimate medical modality using very high quality natural essential oils. Corporate marketing campaigns have turned the meaning of "aromatherapy" into recreational fragrancing, using synthetic chemicals.

Let me give you some background on the medical culture France, beginning with one area of natural medicine that is beginning to grow in the US, namely homeopathy.

I have a good friend and patient, Karen, who lives in a large city in

Virginia, just south of Washington DC. I advised her recently to get some very basic homeopathic remedies at her pharmacy. I was very surprised to find out she had to wait several days before her pharmacist was able to obtain them. The process seemed very complicated.

In France, on the other hand, you would have been able to go to any pharmacy out of 23,000 who stock homeopathic remedies and purchase them immediately, or in a worst case, within an hour or two. This may seem like a whole different medical world, and in fact, it is!

Out of the 60,000 French MDs who practice general medicine, 30,000 or 50% prescribe homeopathic remedies. Out of those 30,000 medical doctors, 83% say they use homeopathy more or less regularly, and 17% have built their practices mainly or exclusively on homeopathy. These doctors are recognized by "L'Ordre des Médecins" (French equivalent of the American Medical Association) our medical licensing organizaton.

In addition to those 30,000 MDs, we can add 2,000 dental surgeons and 700 veterinary doctors who are involved in prescribing homeopathic remedies. Homeopathic prescriptions are covered by our national medical insurance organization. The largest homeopathic laboratory in the world is Boiron, with its Head Office in Lyon. A national opinion pole in 1999 showed that 75% of the French population favors homeopathy and 38% use homeopathic remedies in a regularly.

Clearly, our national medical culture is much more open-minded about using natural healing methods, including nutrition, osteopathy, and the use of plants and essential oils. Thousands of French health professionals in different areas are involved in using essential oilss, including many other MDs. Prescriptions for aromatic preparations written by MDs are prepared by pharmacists and, in many parts of France, most of the cost of these preparations is covered through the national medical insurance organization.

In a reversed perspective, a professional who has a diploma in osteopathy or in chiropractic can legally practice in the US. For NDs (naturopathic doctors), their activity is legal in several states of the US. If you ask me about the situation in France, I have to answer honestly that none of those professions are 'legal' in my country. Does it mean that we cannot consult osteopaths, chiropractors and/or naturopaths ? Not at all! You see, France is well known for its special aptitude in passing so many useless, complicated or even sometimes 'crazy' laws that nobody can abide by them !

If you are an MD in France, everything is open; if you are not an MD, you can do nothing, in theory, from a strict legal point of view. At least, this situation has enabled French MDs to accomplish a highly advanced work in medical aromatherapy. This medical side of aromatherapy was passed to other countries, like for instance Australia and New Zealand, the British Isles, the German speaking countries, Spain and Italy, Israel, and, of course, USA and Canada.

Whenever you encounter anyone anywhere in the world, working seriously in medical aromatherapy, you will find at some point in their training, a connection with the French influence. And, if you check very closely, you will invariably discover a link, directly or indirectly to the ground-breaking laboratory work done by Pierre Franchomme and the subsequent clinical counterpart performed by Dr. Daniel Pénoël.

Our work was published in French in 1990, titled *L'aromathérapie exactement* (Precise Aromatherapy). Though it was translated into Japanese, this work was never published in English, which probably accounts for the lack of awareness of the profound French influence over this new medical science. I give special credit to Pierre Franchomme as my 'aromatic father' and I thank him for his invaluable contribution, in general, to the progress of scientific aromatherapy.

I am indebted to many friends in France with whom I collaborated and from whom I learned much. Quoting a long list of French names is not appropriate for a book published in the US, but I must mention a few. I wish to thank my partner Dominique Davenne, who works on the pharmaceutical and high level cosmetic side of EOs, for his constant support. Even if we do not necessarily share the same views on more subtle and spiritual issues, the links of friendship that connect us can easily go beyond our differing opinions. May he find here the expression of my sincere gratitude.

On the agricultural and distillation side, I thank Michel Meneuvrier, Patrick Collin and Jean-Claude Pichot, who are all engaged in the production of true aromatherapy products, including the implementation of large development programs in very poor countries. Their fundamental work makes our world aromatic program feasible. I wish them all the courage they need for continuing their 'sacred planetary mission' .

I cannot forget our Australian connection and we send our best thoughts to all our friends there, in particular to Ron Guba and his team of collaborators all over Australia and New Zealand. We thank Jim Llewellyn and his wife Robbi Zeck (Melbourne) for helping groups of aromatherapists discover France and experience two-day seminars with us in La Drôme.

In North America, I have many friends who belong to the National Association for Holistic Aromatherapy. They know that I wholeheartedly support their work and I admire the huge progress that has been accomplished within the last few years. I send to all of them collectively my feelings of deep and sincere gratitude. May this simple book help them in their huge teaching, training and informing task for more than 300 million people.

Our special thoughts go to Michael Scholes and Joan Clark, Jeanne Rose, Sylla Sheppard Hanger, John Steele and Kurt Schnaubelt.

More precisely in the context my increased activity in North America, I thank Gary Young who helped us get reconnected there starting in July 1998. He made possible the publication of our first book in English as well as the publication of the proceedings of the 1998 Grasse Symposium on Integrated Aromatic Medicine. His assistance and service to me will never be forgotten.

I also thank Brian Manwaring who edited my first book, and often provides his valuable advice for my other activities in North America. May he find here the expression of my deep thankfulness, which I also extend to his wife Helen, who supports him in such a discrete yet powerful and lovely way. I wish him success in his publishing work to spread this message of hope and action, connected with natural medicine in general and more particularly with aromatic plants and essential oils.

In the perspective of implementing a world-wide aromatic campaign, my thanks go first of all to Ron Williams. His deep intuition that we would collaborate together did find its full confirmation in this New Millenium. He knows how we admire his special talent for harmonizing human relationships and making beautiful things happen in the harsh environment of the commercial world . He is a wonderful example of the 'Dolphin Way' of doing business, and leads his corporation with integrity, sincerity, respect and warmth from the heart. The mutual and reciprocal belief that connects us has the potential to advance the Fourth Aromatic Revolution on a worldwide scale. His understanding of the aromatic 'mission' lies at the core of our collaboration and represents the cornerstone of future successful development. May he find here the expression of our feelings of deep friendship.

I thank Don Tolman for his strong input in helping American people get reconnected with natural nutrition rules and natural hygiene principles. I thank him also for making so many people aware of the importance of the means that Nature uses to speak to us, called the language of signatures. He will discover in reading this book how deeply and accurately those signatures manifest themselves in the world of aromatic plants and essential oils. May our collaboration become a stronger source of inspiration and transformation to an ever growing number of people in North America and worldwide.

To the whole team who supports this project, I send my thankfulness. In particular, to Bill Fifield, Bill Turnbull and all their dedicated co-workers at The Brain Garden in American Fork, Utah.

Rose-Marie and I are especially grateful to all those who have come and attended our seminars. This is the best way for them to get started on the aromatic way and to experience the mental changes that come with new insights. Our mission finds its meaning for and through all of you, working together for the common good.

I thank Mark Burdge and his team at Excel Graphics in Provo, Utah, for once more 'making possible the impossible' so this information could be available for our first US lecture tour in April 2000.
Last and not least, I thank my wife Rose-Marie and our three children, David, Amanda and Magali, for allowing me to spend hundreds of

hours in front of the computer. They all know it is only for the sake of a vital mission.

Finally, I thank all who read this book. I have an important message for you, which will help you, your family and the community around you acquire or regain better control over your health in a wonderful, natural and pleasant way.

Dr Daniel Pénoël
Vallée de la Drôme
March 21, 2000

Chapter 1: By Way of Introduction

The book you are about to read is perhaps one of the most significant of any books I have ever written. Although I have published several volumes that are far more detailed and voluminous about the amazing powers of essential oils on the human body, this one, despite its small size and simplicity, has been two decades in the making. It is different from all my other books, because it was written first in English. Even though my mother tongue is French, I spent some years practicing medicine in Australia, where I was able to begin mastering English. Although I have already published one book in English (*Natural Home Health Care Using Essential Oils*), that one was actually translated from its original French. This one was created from the beginning from English and written especially for the English-speaking countries of the world.

Many of you reading this book may not know anything about me or who I am. So that you may have more confidence in what you are reading and in the instructions and explanations you will find herein, let me tell you briefly about my history.

First of all, I am an MD. I studied at the University of Paris and graduated with a degree in general medicine in 1976. It was important and necessary for me to study conventional, allopathic medicine, but early in my studies I developed a profound conviction in the harmony of nature and in the ability of natural plants to provide health solutions. Even before I graduated, I was convinced that natural methods were, in the long run, more helpful and more effective in helping my patients to regain their health and stay healthy. My wife, Rose-Marie, whom I met in my third year of medical school, was intuitively attracted to these natural methods, and to the use of plant-based medicines, rather than synthetic drugs.

I began my practice near Paris, and immediately incorporated natural methods in treating my patients. Initially, these included homeopathy and acupuncture, which I had studied in parallel with my conventional medical training. I had very good results adding these complementary methods to my practice, but early in my career I also discovered essential oils. I found that I could get significantly better results in healing my patients when essential oils were included in the treatment. Both my patients and I were often amazed at their effectiveness. In France, we refer to the use of essential oils for healing as "aromathérapie." We think of this as a form of medicine. My impressions are that most North Americans think of aromatherapy as nothing more than pleasant odors for relaxation. You must remember that when I talk of "aromatherapy," using the English word, for me it is a true form of life-giving medicine, not just fancy air freshening.

Since 1977, I have made essential oils a cornerstone of my practice. I have lectured all over the world and have become somewhat of a spokesperson for these amazing medicinal substances. I have used them in my clinic for more than 23 years, during which time I have learned a great deal about how they work and how they strengthen and heal the human body.

In 1990, in partnership with a fellow scientist, Pierre Franchomme, a French biochemist, we published the first medical reference guide on using essential oils. It was written in French and titled, *L'aromatherapie exactement* or, in English, "Precise Aromatherapy." In this book, we integrated my clinical experience with Pierre's biochemical understandings and outlined the medical properties of hundreds of essential oils. This book is still being used all over the world by scientists and health professionals who are beginning to discover the healing powers of essential oils.

I know that most North Americans are not at all familiar with essential oils. So it was a little difficult for me to write this book, primarily because I had to back up and address myself to an audience that was just beginning to discover the potential and nature of essential oils.

I found the solution for doing this was to consider my patients who had never before encountered essential oils and try to present answers to the questions that they asked. As you read this book, I hope you will be able to feel that we are talking together in my office. I am going to try to anticipate all the questions that new patients ask and share with you much information on how to use essential oils effectively to improve and protect your health and the health of your family members.

Although English is not my mother tongue, I have tried hard to share the spirit of love and respect that I have for all human beings and for nature. I am continually in awe at the benevolence and power that plants have to help the human organism. I see natural medicine, and aromatherapy (in the French sense of the word) as the wave of the future in bringing a new level of health and vitality, not only to our bodies, but also to our minds, our societies and the whole earth environment. I hope you will be able to sense that spirit of reverence in my words as we learn together about the amazing therapeutic world of essential oils.

Chapter 2: What Are Essential Oils and Why Are They So Powerful?

Most people find that their first experience with essential oils is very positive, but that is only partly due to their typically pleasant aromas. Rarely do I encounter a patient who does not notice an immediate increase in well being when they first use essential oils. Unfortunately, many do not have the faintest idea where these volatile oils come from. To help explain this I will give you a little background in what I would call 'overall basic physical chemistry.'

When I ask my patients what "oils" they are familiar with, I usually hear one of the following:

1. One or more common vegetable oils such as corn oil, olive oil, saf flower oils, etc.
2. One or more mineral oils, such as lubricating oil, petroleum jelly, or motor oil.

I then ask, "Do any of these oils exist naturally in that state?" Most realize immediately that oils are almost always created through some form of extracting and/or refining process. With vegetable oils, such as olive oil or sunflower oil, the oil is obtained through pressure. The oil is literally squeezed from the fruit or the seeds. In agribusiness, where there is minimal concern for wholeness and organic quality, heat and chemical solvents are used to significantly increase the yield. However, this damages the chemical structure of the oils. The highest quality vegetable oils are always "cold-pressed" in that only pressure is used to extract the oil. Heat and solvents are not used and the natural, beneficial chemical structure of the oil remains relatively intact.

Mineral oils and lubricating oils are distilled or refined from crude oil. This process separates or fractions the oils into progressively finer compounds, with the least-refined being the heaviest and the most-refined being the lightest.

In both cases we are talking about a process of extraction, meaning that something is taken out of another thing. An extraction process is the basis for most of our primary industries. Mining is perhaps the best known example, where pure metal is extracted from very large amounts of ore. Through extraction processes we get rid of unnecessary substances, and isolate in concentrated, pure form, the substances that we are seeking. In essential oil extraction—as in mining—a great deal of plant material must be distilled in order to create small, concentrated amounts of the desired product. The more raw product required to create the substance, the more costly the process and the more valuable the end result.

The power of this distillation process and of the effect of concentration is well illustrated by a magnifying glass. A sheet of paper can be placed under a hot sun and sit for hours without showing any damage. But as soon as a magnifying glass is placed between the sun and the paper, and held at a proper distance to concentrate the sun's rays on a small point, the paper will quickly begin to smoke and then burn. The radiant energy of the sun is concentrated onto a small pinpoint of area.

Concentration is a vital principle and is all around us. In engineering, for example, pressure, tension, torsion and shear forces are concentrated on specific supporting members of stable structures. In our minds also, we use mental concentration and focus to try to improve our performance in athletic, scholastic, and economic endeavors.

It is very important to understand that essential ois are extremely concentrated. Let me illustrate with some of the oils we will present in this handbook. To produce 10-ml (1/3 oz.) of essential oil of peppermint, for example, 3-4 pounds of fresh plant material are required. Many essential oils require much more plant material. Twelve to fourteen pounds of plant material are required to produce a 10-ml bottle of geranium essential oil! So, you can understand that even a single drop of essential oil represents dozens of stalks of plant material.

There is evidence that aromatic plants were being steam-distilled for their essences long before the time of Christ. I won't elaborate on the ancient history here, but by the fifteenth century, steam distillation of aromatic plants was widespread throughout Europe.

The process is fairly simple. Fresh plant material, harvested at the right time, is loaded into a watertight chamber. Some commercial essential oil distilleries can process hundreds of pounds of plant material in a single batch. When the chamber is loaded, steam enters the chamber from the bottom and rises through the plant material. As it does so, it liberates special fragrant substances within the plant material, and these aromatic compounds or essences rise with the steam. The steam leaves the chamber and enters a condensing coil, where it cools back to water.

Because it does not dissolve in water and is lighter than water, the precious aromatic fluid that came from the plants floats on top of the condensed water and is easily removed. This special substance which floats on top is the "essential oil" and can contain hundreds of complex compounds. The condensed water underneath, also contains some water-soluble aromatic compounds, though not nearly as concentrated, and is referred to as "floral water."

There are dozens of different variables that must be precisely controlled in order to extract essential oils that have therapeutic value. The quality of the growing environment, the nutrients in the soil, the time of plant harvest, the amount of time between harvest and distillation, the duration and pressure of the steam, the quality of the still, and proper storage of the essential oil after distillation.... all of these factors can destroy the quality of the resulting essential oil and make it ineffective for therapy, even though it may smell very good.

It takes highly skilled and knowledgeable people to control and monitor the entire process in a way that produces essential oils that have the therapeutic power of the ones in my kits. Very high quality essential oils can cost as much as 20 times more than low quality, inexpensively grown and distilled essential oils.

Unfortunately–and I can't stress this point enough–most of the essential oils imported to North America in the past few decades have been produced primarily for flavor or fragrance, and not for therapeutic use. There are major differences in quality among them. Additionally, oils that are produced only for flavorings and fragrance are often diluted and extended with additives that can be harmful if used for therapy.

Now let's turn to peppermint essential oil as an example. Peppermint essential oil contains menthol, among other things, which has an immediate and powerful cooling effect on the skin. It is very effective for relieving pain from bumps and bruises, or what we doctors call minor trauma. We're talking of injuries that can cause a lot of pain, but don't require hospital treatment.

A very common form of minor trauma is a hard bump on the shin. This area can be extremely sensitive since the bone is just under the skin. One of the most dramatic ways of demonstrating the effectiveness of essential oils is to apply just two drops of peppermint essential oil to the bumped area. Apply the drops with the dropper, then spread the oil by tapping lightly with a finger (preferably the little finger) around and onto the painful area. The pain usually subsides amazingly quickly.

A second step to further improve results in treating a bump or bruise, one can place two drops of peppermint oil in a bottle (6 oz) of cold water, seal with a lid, and shake well. Soak a cloth or paper towel with this aromatic hydric suspension to create a compress. Apply the wet paper towel to the painful area and then cover it with a layer of cling wrap for a few hours. In the vast majority of cases, this two step treatment with peppermint essential oil will (1) immediately reduce or nearly eliminate the pain, (2) prevent or reduce the amount of bruising, and (3) leave the bumped area feeling much less tender after the compress is removed.

Peppermint essential oil can also relieve common stomach distress and nausea. I have frequently brought complete relief to myself or a friend by merely inhaling its stimulating aroma or by putting a trace on a finger and touching the finger to the tongue.

But, as you probably already realize, in order to use essential oils on these everyday problems, they must be ready and easily at hand. For this reason, I strongly recommend that you fill small bottles (1-2 ml) of several varieties of essential oils and place them in a little carrying kit for your purse, or your car, or attached to your belt (as I do it). I call this a "microkit," and I keep it with me all the time. As my wife, Rose-Marie, and I travel all over the world, my microkit is constantly in use, not only for emergencies, but also for everyday refreshment and health.

The example of the trauma to the shin illustrates three important characteristics of essential oils that make them so useful:

1) they are highly concentrated
2) they are easy to apply because they are in liquid form
3) because of their molecular structure, they absorb quickly into and through body tissues. Aromatic molecules are both very active (volatile) and are liposoluble, enabling them to rapidly penetrate cell walls and enter the blood stream.

Imagine what it would be like to try to rub peppermint leaves on the shin bruise, rather than using the essential oil? It would be very uncomfortable, messy and inefficient. You would have to rub a pound or more of peppermint leaves on the shin to get a fraction of the phytochemicals that a few drops of the essential oil provide!

This might seem like a crazy example, but I want you to grasp through this comparison how dramatically different it is to use the essential oil of an aromatic plant rather than using the plant itself.

One of the reasons essential oils hold so much potential for therapy (and also why they should be studied as a separate form of healing, distinct from actual herbal plants) is that they do enter the body tissues so rapidly and effectively. This enables them to bring about quick results, whether it be in reducing pain, stimulating circulation, strengthening body systems or relieving congestion.

Though France has historically played a major role in the initial development of the therapeutic use of essential oils, English-speaking countries are rapidly embracing these new health-giving substances. I am convinced that the United States—as it so often does in other scientific/economic developments—will ultimately play a leadership role in bringing essential oil therapy (what I call Integrated Aromatic Medicine) into the mainstream of the healing profession.

The more I study and use essential oils, the more I comprehend the long-range ramifications of using therapies provided by Nature, rather than by a laboratory at a chemical corporation. The impact of this paradigm shift in health care is unfathomable. This handbook can only scratch the surface, but it will help you begin a rewarding journey.

In the pages that follow, I will first discuss the subject of safety. The high concentration of essential oils mandates that they be used with care and wisdom. After the section on safety, we will examine together, in individual chapters, the uses and applications of each of the eight single essential oils that are contained in my singles kit. Once we have covered that indispensable knowledge, I will briefly explain the purpose and wonderful synergy in creating essential oil blends. Then I will continue with the uses and applications of five blends that I have included in my first blends kit. These blends were created to enable you to provide sound maintenance for your body as well as your mind.

Chapter 3: The All-Important Rules of Safety

Any instruction on the uses and applications of specific essential oils and blends would be incomplete and irresponsible without a beginning section on the safety precautions that must be taken in order to have a positive and successful experience with essential oils. You should not attempt to use therapeutic essential oils until you have carefully read and understood this safety section. Essential oils must be treated with respect. To emphasize the importance of these guidelines, I have listed them in summary form on the inside cover of this book.

Because of the super concentrated state of pure essential oils, only very small amounts are required in application. This is a difficult concept for some people. I like to say that "less is more" with essential oils. Sometimes just the right amount of an essential oil is no more than a tiny trace on a fingertip.

Let me illustrate this by discussing salt. In seawater, this salt concentration is about 1 oz. per quart, but when the water is evaporated, it can be collected in its pure crystalline form. In this highly concentrated form it is much easier to transport and use in seasoning. In cooking, salt is never used in the same volume as flour or even sugar. Salt in food needs to be diluted.

Similarly, no one would take a teaspoon of salt and pour it directly into the mouth! No one would think of putting salt directly in contact with the eyes! No one would pour salt on an open wound!

Just like salt, essential oils typically are diluted in vegetable oils for more convenient, safer application. Yet there is still good reason for providing essential oils in their fully concentrated or "neat" state. By so doing, we have the option of adjusting the concentration to fit the need, significantly increasing the number of potential essential oil applications. It is the same with salt. You would not always want to buy it or use it in a highly diluted form. You want to have the flexibility to adjust the concentration.

I mention here eleven basic safety guidelines. The first four concern avoiding or negating burns from essential oils. The second four concern specific cautions for specific types of oils and persons. The last three are general cautionary steps that should always be taken when using essential oils.

A. Essential oils <u>cannot</u> dissolve in water. Trying to reduce the irritation caused by some essential oils on the skin with water can actually make the situation worse.

It is impossible to dilute essential oils or reduce their impact on sensitive skin, by using water. In fact, using water on essential oils is like trying to put out a gasoline fire with water: it can actually make the fire worse!

The substances that can and will dilute essential oils and reduce the burning sensation, are vegetable oils. You should always have some vegetable oil present when applying essential oils. So here are the first four guidelincs. . .

B. Essential oils <u>can</u> be diluted in vegetable oil. Always keep some high quality vegetable oil handy when using essential oils.

Any good essential oil kit must contain a bottle of quality vegetable oil for dilution. In all the workshops Rose-Marie and I teach in France, we insist that those who create a kit of essential oils for natural home health care—including a microkit—include a bottle of high quality vegetable oil for practical and safety reasons. Any irritation caused by an essential oil has to be buffered with an appropriate liquid substance that can dilute, soothe and relieve the burning pain. The liquid that mixes thoroughly with essential oils in any proportion, is high quality vegetable oil.

I have created a special blend of grapeseed, sweet almond and sesame oils for the singles kit, which provides an excellent medium for diluting essential oils.

C. Never allow essential oils in their fully concentrated (neat) state to come in contact with mucous membranes or sensitive skin areas.

Very commonly someone applies essential oils using their fingers, to the feet or chest or some other part of the body and then a few minutes later, forgetting there is essential oil residue on their fingers, they rub their eyes! This will almost certainly create irritation, sometimes severe, in the eyes. Other times, a more serious situation arises when pouring an essential oil, and a drop accidentally splashes directly into the eye. In this case the pain can be intense. The essential oil must be diluted immediately. I advise using almond oil, if available, which is the mildest for the eyes, but any pure vegetable oil will help. Put it on a cotton ball and delicately dab at the eye.

Anyone who has seen me teach has observed that when I apply essential oils, I use my little finger rather than the index finger to do so. I am often questioned why I put my little finger over the vial opening to receive a trace of oil and then apply with that little finger. It feels much more natural to use the index finger, they insist. But it is expressly for that reason that I train my students to use the little finger: it is then much less likely that that finger will accidentally be used to rub an eye or scratch the skin! Also, it is easier to apply smaller amounts of essential oil, using the little finger.

D. Never add undiluted (neat) essential oils directly to bath water. Use bath salts to disperse them.

As you know, essential oils cannot mix with water, so when they are added directly to bath water, they float on top. The skin around the genital area is some of the most sensitive skin on the body. If neat essential oils are added to bath water, the chances are good that a person entering the bath will have one of the most unpleasant experiences of his/her life!

I am amazed, particularly in the United States, at the limited amount of information on how to safely use essential oils. Many of my students, some of whom have been using essential oils for years, come up to me after a seminar and comment that they have never before heard of so many ways to avoid problems and insure a safe and positive experience.

Here are a few questions often asked me:

1. In case someone accidentally swallows neat essential oil, should they swallow vegetable oil?

Yes, I advise taking a swallow or two of pure, quality vegetable oil. This plays a double function. First, it soothes the irritation of the mucous membranes in the esophagus. Second, it will slow down the penetration of the essential oil directly into the bloodstream through the stomach wall. The presence of the lipids in the vegetable oil triggers the digestive process. The vegetable oil both dilutes the essential oil molecules and carries them into the alimentary canal, preventing quick absorption through the stomach wall. I am speaking here of minor incidents. In cases of massive ingestion (more than a teaspoon), vegetable oil will offer some protection, but immediate professional care should also be obtained.

2. If essential oils cannot be added directly to bath water, how then does one take an aromatic bath?

It is very simple. Mix 10 drops of essential oil thoroughly into 2-3 tablespoons of salt. The salt/essential oil mixture can then be added to the bathwater, either directly or by using a flow-through bag. Of the eight single oils in your kit, any of the oils can be used in a bath, except peppermint, because the menthol makes it too 'cold.' We don't often use tropical basil in baths, because it smells more like cooking in a kitchen than an aromatic bath! The rule is never pour essential oil directly into the bath.

3. I have heard of mixing essential oils in drinking water. How can I do this if essential oils cannot mix with water?

It is true that essential oils cannot mix with water, but you can flavor your water with a trace of essential oil. When I use the term 'trace' I am speaking of a quantity smaller than a drop, an amount you might obtain by touching your finger to the lip of an essential oil vial and mixing it in the water. An easy way to put a 'trace' in a glass of water is to dip the end of a toothpick in the essential oil and then stir it into a glass of drinking water.

One drop is really too much to mix in a single glass of water, but it can be mixed in a glass of fresh orange or apple juice. If possible, use freshly squeezed or centrifuged juice, so you will have all the vitamins and enzymes. These fresh juice/essential oil mixtures can be vitalizing and purifying beverages, which are very quickly absorbed by the stomach. These should not, however, be taken with meals. It is best if these drinks are consumed at least 30 minutes before a meal. We will provide some aromatic drink recipes in later chapters.

4. What about preparing natural, herbal teas with essential oils?

These are delightful drinks and very soothing to the digestive, respiratory and nervous systems. All the oils in your singles kit can be used in a warm tea, because I have specifically selected some of the safest essential oils for that kit. These teas are prepared by placing a spoonful of natural honey in a cup, then placing one or two drops of essential oil on the honey and mixing thoroughly with a toothpick or chopstick. The honey changes slightly when the essential oil is mixed in it. Pour warm (not hot) water over the honey/essential oil mixture while stirring. In just a few seconds you have a delicious and healthy aromatic tea, ready for drinking.

I suggest balsam fir and *Eucalyptus radiata* teas for soothing a cough. Lemon or peppermint or a lemon/peppermint combination tastes delicious and helps an upset stomach or congested liver. Tropical basil can be used to help stomach and intestinal function.

There are some essential oils—not included in my kit—rich in phenols, which contain very powerful and highly irritating aromatic molecules. These include savory, oregano, and thyme. Likewise, the cinnamic aldehyde found in cinnamon bark essential oil is too aggressive to be used in honey teas. These oils should NOT be used as described above. They must first be significantly diluted in vegetable oil. If you stick to the oils provided in the kit, you should have no problems.

The second set of four guidelines focuses on special precautions to take for specific oils being used in specific situations.

E. People with allergies must be very cautious with essential oils.

An allergic reaction can occur even when using a very high quality essential oil. It all depends on the body chemistry of the person using the oil. Always ask about allergies. If the person—or any members of his/her family—has known allergies to anything, extra precautions should be taken. If there has ever been any manifestation of asthma or hay fever in the respiratory system, or eczema or hives, then there is a greater potential for an allergic reaction to essential oils. It does not necessarily mean that essential oils should not be used, but that they must be used with greater caution.

The essential oils should be tested first on the skin area of the body that has the least likelihood of reaction. That is the skin on the soles of the feet. Even when used neat, essential oils are not likely to trigger reactions on the feet. To avoid problems, where allergies are suspected, we always apply essential oils through the soles of the feet, rather than on other, more sensitive areas. In so doing, we are not trying to give a foot massage, but rather using the less sensitive foot areas as an absorption point. Essential oils are quickly absorbed into the body, and aromatic molecules are carried through the bloodstream relatively quickly to all parts and organs in the body. It takes a bit more time for essential oils to be absorbed through the feet, but it does work and it is a way to apply essential oils while greatly reducing the likelihood of skin irritation or reaction.

If there is a history of respiratory allergies, essential oils should not be breathed close to aerosol devices or electric diffusers. Topical applications should be made at locations other than the throat and chest. Here again, the soles of the feet provide the safest option.

F. Essential oils rich in menthol should not be used close to the throat or neck on children under 30 months of age.

This special safety rule that is applied with pharmaceutical products should also be used with essential oils, and it applies particularly to peppermint essential oil because of its menthol content. The reason for this rule is that there can be a risk of laryngeal spasm when menthol is applied near a young child's throat.

G. Some citrus essential oils are light sensitizing, so exposure to sun must be avoided for 24 hours after application.

Some essential oils, particularly from the citrus family, have the potential for making the skin highly sensitive to the sun's rays. These oils should never be used on skin that will be directly exposed to the sun. Lemon is the only citrus oil in my kit NOT obtained through steam distillation. Instead this oil is obtained through a mechanical pressing process that literally squeezes essential oil out of lemon rinds. Technically this substance is called an 'essence' as opposed to an 'essential oil.' If the lemon rinds had been steam distilled, yielding essential oil, there would be no risk of photosensitization. But since they are 'cold pressed' a category of molecules is preserved in the essential oil called furocoumarins.

If the lemon essential oil is applied on skin exposed directly to the sun's rays, there is a risk of reaction with the UV rays, which can result in brown spots on the skin. Avoid sun exposure for at least 24 hours after applying any cold-pressed citrus essential oil.

Many ask if this same precaution applies to artificial UV exposure received in tanning booths. The answer is emphatically yes! In fact, the tanning booths involve even more risk because of their higher concentration of UV rays.

H. Some essential oils have strong caustic characteristics and should be avoided or only used very cautiously and only in diluted form.

There are some relatively common essential oils which have caustic characteristics which must be used with utmost care, and always in diluted form, unless under the direction of a qualified health professional. These essential oils contain compounds that are so strong that they can burn the skin. Examples include the phenol-rich thyme, oregano, savory, and clove; cinnamon leaf and cinnamon bark essential oil rich in cinnamic aldehyde; and lemongrass with a concentration of citrals. All of these oils have the potential to create painful burns even when used in small amounts, and should be avoided. Of course, none of them are found in your singles kit.

I. Care must be taken to tightly close all essential oil bottles after use.

J. Always store essential oil vials in a safe, cool place out of reach of children, and out of direct sunlight

These two obvious, but very important safety considerations apply in all cases of essential oil use. While these are clearly self-evident, my wife and I always stress these last two points because they are easily forgotten and, if overlooked, may result in serious problems.

The last rule applies to severe acute situations. When experiencing an excess of energy, such as a severe inflammation of a joint (the area is congested, reddish, hot), applying neat essential oils will 'add fuel to the fire.' The energy of the oils will combine with the inflammatory energy. Not only is there no benefit, but usually it will aggravate the inflammation and increase the pain!

So, the eleventh safety rule is the following one:

K. Do not apply neat essential oils on areas of the body that are inflamed (usually hot, red, swollen and tender).

The best remedy in these cases is an aromatic compress soaked with highly diluted essential oils strongly dispersed in cold water or cold floral water, to help remove the 'heat' as well as heal the tissues.

These eleven safety precautions are listed on the inside cover of this handbook. Refer to them often so they will be permanently imprinted on your mind. Now that we have covered them, we are prepared to begin a most fascinating and interesting journey of discovery. I will review with you each of the eight single essential oils explaining in detail how they can benefit and enrich your life and the lives of your family members.

Chapter 4: Introduction to Single Oils

The goal of this book is NOT to make you doctors, nurses or professional aromatherapists. My intent is to give you simple and practical steps to use essential oils effectively in your home. So much of what essential oils can do is very straightforward and simple. I will present several principles of self-care that anyone can master for himself or herself without having to consult a doctor.

There are many occasions when a health care professional is necessary, and what I present is not intended to supercede or eliminate that need. I will be discussing what can be done with essential oils as simple, first-aid measures for very common incidents and health problems. I do not want this information to prevent or discourage you in any way from seeking professional health advice when it is needed. When it comes to serious problems, nothing can replace the advice of your doctor.

Symptoms alone are not always sufficient to make a correct diagnosis. A complete and correct diagnosis is the crucial first step in fixing any health problem. If the initial diagnosis is wrong, the treatment protocol will almost inevitably be wrong also.

We can use an analogy with car repair. When the engine is not running smoothly, a mechanic may diagnose the problem as a bad spark plug. But if the real problem is a faulty spark plug wire, replacing the plug will actually have little or no effect. Every year in the United States, more than 80,000 people die because of incorrect diagnoses. It is a serious problem worldwide.

Nature has provided us with many excellent answers for treating many problems. We may disagree with a chemical prescription for solving the problem, but the critical question is to correctly isolate the problem first. Health professionals are trained and equipped to make those determinations in unusual or serious or emergency situations.

Still, I believe it is correct for us to take responsibility for the daily routines that will improve our health. And on this point the pendulum is swinging the other way. For a long time we have entrusted our doctors and hospitals with total responsibility for our health. Now we are realizing that we as individuals must carry much of the responsibility for how we eat, sleep, work and think. I am delighted to see this paradigm shift take place. I have an accountant who experienced some serious problems with his car. A faulty 'diagnosis' and an incorrect repair by his mechanic resulted in a car problem that endangered his life. He decided then to learn car repair for himself and since that time has done most of his own repairs. By knowing enough to make corrections early, when problems are minor, we can often avoid having to struggle as much with the truly major problems.

It is not my intent here to create a large reference guide. I will be explaining many principles and experiences with each of these separate chapters on the oils, and my hope is that you will read through all of them to glean all of the information I have to share. Each chapter builds on the previous one.

Essential oil therapy is a relatively new topic for modern medicine. My foundation training, in medical school, was hard science, and I became fully satisfied that there was plenty of scientific evidence for using essential oils to treat health problems. However, as I have experienced the healing powers of essential oils in my clinical practice for over 20 years, I have also experienced what is referred to as the 'subtle' powers of essential oils. These include the power of essential oils to enhance our emotional and spiritual well being as well as our physical well being. It is an area that is impossible to evaluate through hard science, though I have experienced it on many occasions. My term 'integrated aromatic medicine' includes both types of essential oil influences.

Most doctors will tell you that a major percentage of the problems they treat are either caused by or heavily influenced by psychological factors. How fitting then, that essential oils, with documented health-enhancing powers, also carry with them—through their stimulating, calming or balancing aromas—strong influences for favorably affecting psychological factors, as well.

Lastly, please understand that essential oil therapy is an exercise in learning and doing, as well as reading and study. Most of the knowledge Rose-Marie and I have to share has been gained through experience. So when I make a recommendation to you for safety's sake or for proper usage, please do not take it lightly.

Now let's begin the exciting journey of learning how to use each of these eight wonderful essential oils.

Chapter 5: Peppermint *(Mentha piperita)*

When selecting the eight oils for your singles kit, peppermint was the first and easiest choice. It cannot be replaced by any other essential oil, because of its unique characteristics. For me, it is a must in any aromatic kit. It is primarily produced in the northern United States.

Pain from Trauma

There are several important uses for peppermint, and we will start with the most common one, namely pain from a blow or bruise (local trauma). Peppermint contains a large amount of menthol and because of that molecule, it has a strong cooling effect on the skin. It is this cooling process that controls pain so quickly, in a way similar to the effect of a cold compress.

You should remember, however, that all essential oils contain a multiplicity of aromatic compounds, and it is an amazing thing to see how they work in conjunction with each other, or rather in synergy with each other. In other words, nature has blended chemicals in essential oils which are 'synergistic,' meaning they are mixed in the right amounts to create greater healing power than if they existed separately. There are other compounds in peppermint besides menthol, and it is these additional compounds that make peppermint essential oil more effective than using menthol alone.

About 10 years ago, we vacationed in southern France with Rose-Marie's mother. During the trip, my mother-in-law's hand was seriously crushed by the sliding panel door on our van. Her pain was excruciating! Fortunately, I had my aromatic kit, as always, in the glove box. I took the peppermint essential oil and immediately applied several drops to the traumatized area. Within a minute or two, the pain was under control. I carefully wrapped the hand in gauze and bandaged it. I later used other complementary essential oils (including helichrysum) to bring about complete healing. But only peppermint has the capacity to reduce pain in such a short time.

When you apply peppermint to a trauma in the first few seconds you help break the vicious cycle of pain leading to inflammation, which often leads to more pain, etc. But even when you cannot apply the peppermint immediately it can still be helpful. Michel, our primary lavender distiller in the Drome valley, bruised his foot while working, and when he returned home that day a few hours later, he was still feeling the pain. He had some peppermint essential oil at home, so he applied a few drops and felt a significant reduction in pain, even though the injury had occurred several hours earlier. Immediate application is the best procedure, but a delayed application can still prove useful.

Another incident occurred with a worker who was injured trying to remove an old fireplace from our living room. He was using a large hammer to loosen the bricks, and accidentally missed the structure, striking his knee! His pain was so intense he nearly fainted. Fortunately, Rose Marie rushed in with the bottle of peppermint essential oil and applied several drops to the knee. His knee was still throbbing after a few minutes, so she applied the oil a second time. Ten minutes later, she applied the peppermint a third time. By this time he was feeling so much better that he actually began working again!

In a situation like this, you should get an X-ray to be sure there is no break or crack in the kneecap. For safety's sake is it is better to get the X-ray and find nothing wrong, than to neglect it and miss the diagnosis and proper treatment. Peppermint is capable of reducing the pain to such an extent that one might not fully realize the seriousness his/her injury.

While peppermint can be a wonderful aid in reducing pain and avoiding inflammation, it is not necessarily sufficient by itself to heal the trauma. In my earlier English book, *Natural Home Health Care Using Essential Oils,* I related an experience I had after knocking my shin with a piece of lumber while gardening. In areas like the shin, where the bone is close to the skin, the body may sometimes react to trauma by forming tiny, crystal-like, nodules. These are not felt at first, but they reveal their soreness later, if the traumatized area is touched, even lightly. Their existence creates something like a 'dam' on the circulation of energy along the energy pathways known as "meridians" in Eastern medicine. It is important that these nodules be dissolved in order for complete healing to take place. I used a small rolling/massaging device known as a facial spirex, which I have found to be very effective in my practice. This device is only manufactured in France, but hopefully, it can someday be produced in the US. Otherwise, this congestion can be alleviated by light hand massage.

These complications from trauma are of particular interest to me because I have studied many branches of natural medicine and also energy medicine. In particular, these approaches help us perceive the body as a whole, that all its parts are interconnected, both mentally and physically. By this I mean that an unpleasant incident that occurred ten years ago, whether physical or psychological, may influence health problems in the present. Similarly, an incident that takes place today may determine the location or nature of future problems…. even though a Western-minded doctor might never recognize the link! For example, a lady we know who distills lavender in the high mountains near our home told us that she lost her husband due to bone cancer that appeared on his femur at exactly the site where a male goat had kicked him a few years earlier.

So it is important not only to relieve the pain (symptom), but also to heal the wound (cause). Peppermint addresses the pain problem, but what further aromatic care should you use to bring about healing?

Here I will introduce the concept of essential oil blends. You have in your kit some oils that are very effective when blended together for specific purposes. Blending essential oils enables us to combine the healing aromatic molecules from multiple essential oils to create a substance that has more healing power than the ingredient oils would have separately. This is the principle of synergy: the effect of the combined oils is greater than the effect of the oils used individually. In fact, in France, we refer to essential oil blends as 'synergies.'

In a mixing vial, combine

- 5 drops of lavender
- 4 drops of balsam fir
- 4 drops of lemon
- 3 drops of geranium
- 1 teaspoon of carrier oil

Gently massage the injured area with this blend. Then create a compress by pouring 4-5 drops of this same blend into a separate vial with 4 tsp. of water. Seal the vial and shake vigorously. (The oil and water, of course, will not mix, but the oil will disperse within the water into very tiny droplets.) Pour the water mixture onto a saucer and quickly place in it a length of gauze sufficient to wrap the injured area. Then wrap the wet gauze around the injured area and follow this by wrapping the whole area with a clear cling film. The cling film can then be covered with another dry gauze or bandage. This should kept in place for an hour or two, and can be kept overnight, and can be repeated as needed.

If you happen to have my blends kit in addition to the singles kit, you can simplify the procedure as follows:

1. Gently massage directly over the trauma area 5 drops of my calming blend mixed with 15 drops of carrier oil.
2. Massage the surrounding muscles using 5 drops of my exercise blend mixed with 15 drops of carrier oil.
3. Make the compress as instructed using the calming blend.

To summarize then, on the issue of pain due to a trauma such as a bump or bruise:

A. Apply a few drops of peppermint to the injured area as soon as possible to relieve pain and help reduce inflammation.
B. Use additional oils to help speed the healing process, using gentle massage and compresses.
C. If the trauma is serious, seek diagnosis from a qualified health professional, even if the peppermint seems to eliminate the pain.

Headache Pain

Now I want to deal with one of our most common sources of pain. Headaches are symptoms of something else that is wrong in the organism. We can temporarily relieve this symptom with aspirin, acetaminophen, ibuprofen and other commercial painkillers. We can also use a natural approach with peppermint essential oil, which I will shortly explain. But to eliminate headaches entirely requires a deeper and more serious protocol. To be successful you have to implement and follow a full program of new mental, physical and dietary exercises—something we call a body/mind program.

A. Headaches away from home.
To relieve a headache one needs only a trace of peppermint applied to each temple and the center of the forehead. This should be done as soon as the headache begins. (A trace means less than a drop, acquired on the little finger by touching it to the edge of the essential oil bottle or dropper.) **Important caution:** when applying peppermint to the forehead or temples, take extra care to be sure no essential oil gets near the eyes. Because of the menthol in peppermint, even a trace in the eyes can be very painful.

Additionally, you should massage the back of the neck with diluted lavender (5 drops to 1 teaspoon of carrier oil), taking particular care to massage the muscles in the nape of the neck with a downward movement. Lavender can also be used neat on the ear lobes (the lobes represent the reflex point for the head in auricular (ear) reflexology.

Lastly, if the headache is accompanied by digestive congestion, an herbal tea, made with a drop of lavender or peppermint mixed in a half teaspoon of honey and diluted with warm water, will help in a deeper way, from the inside.

B. Headaches at home.
When headaches occur at home, where you can apply a compress to the head, do the following:

Step 1: Massage the back of the neck in downward strokes using 5 drops of lavender in a teaspoon of carrier oil.

Step 2: Apply a wet compress to the head as follows: Mix one drop of peppermint and three drops of lavender with 4 tsp. of water in a vial. Seal the vial, shake vigorously and pour onto a saucer. Soak a 12' piece of gauze, loosely rolled, in this liquid, and then wrap completely around the head—forehead, temples parietals and occiput—several times. Then place a layer of cling film around the gauze, and finally a dry bandage over the cling film. Then lie in bed in a dark room for 30 to 60 minutes.

C. Chronic headaches
If headaches are chronic, meaning they are a continual problem in a person's life, you will need to follow a complete detoxification program. I remember well the case of one woman who came to me for

help with some very large and serious leg ulcers. These open ulcers oozed pus daily. She wanted to know if essential oils could heal the ulcers. She also mentioned that whenever her allopathic doctor had managed to close the ulcers, in an artificial way using only drugs—not paying any attention to the lifestyle that had created the problem—she always experienced unbearable migraine headaches! She was a classic example of what we call in natural medicine "morbid transfer." This means that when one part of the body is cured, without getting to the root cause of the problem, then another part of the body becomes ill.

It is because of the problem of morbid transfer that I refuse to use essential oils in a way that I consider allopathic and not naturopathic. By this I mean that I will not prescribe essential oils, if I know that there are fundamental causes for a disease inherent in lifestyle or diet habits. In the case of this particular patient, I learned by asking a few questions about her diet, that she was addicted to eating the wrong foods. It was her regular habit to consume enormous quantities of white bread, cheese and pasta. It was clear to me that the substance oozing from her giant ulcers was directly linked with her junk food dict. Attempting to suppress this unnatural form of elimination without changing her dietary habits would be potentially harmful to her life. The body had to get rid of the toxic mucous her diet was creating, so it found a way through the ulcers. Unfortunately, as I mentioned, her need for these junk foods had become a controlling addiction and she was unwilling to consider changing it. That was the end of our consultation and as far as I know she never did solve her ulcer problem.

Cautions concerning burns

I am often asked this question: "If peppermint is so effective at cooling and relieving a trauma, why not apply neat peppermint essential oil to a burn? It could seem logical that the cooling effect would be beneficial for a minor burn. However, following the principles of energy medicine, a trauma is an area characterized by stagnation of the blood (bruise) resulting in an accumulation of "cold" energy (black and blue). A burn on the other hand results in an increase of blood circulation (redness and inflammation) and results in an oversupply of 'hot" energy. Thus a burn and a bump are energetically opposite. Essential oils in their fully concentrated state bring substantial amounts of energy into the organism, and when applied to an injury that is already highly inflamed or hot—as in a burn—they can aggravate the inflammation.

A more effective approach would be to use the cold water compress discussed earlier. Again, we are not creating a solution, since the essential oils are not water soluble, but when mixed with water and shaken vigorously, we create a rough suspension of the essential oils in water and this coarse mixture is sufficient for in-home treatment with a compress (i.e. soaked in a gauze and wrapped with cling film.)

So I do not recommend immediately applying neat essential oils to a burn. It is true—as we have all heard—that René-Maurice Gattefossé did accidentally plunge his burned hand into a vat of neat lavender essential oil, and found that it brought substantial relief and rapid healing.

But given the strength of essential oils, it is more practical to use a diluted form for burns, at least for those minor burns that occur frequently at home.

It is still true that one of the most important steps is to remove the heat from the burn. Where possible it is always advisable to run cold tap water over the burn area, 10 minutes being the usual recommended time. Once this has been done, then apply the following water/ essential oil compress as recommended by Shirley Price, a very good friend of ours and a well-known English aromatherapist:

> Mix five drops of lavender and one drop of peppermint in 4 tsp. of water. Seal in a vial and shake vigorously. Soak an appropriate length of gauze in this mixture and wrap the burn, then cover it with cling film and a dry bandage. It is helpful to further apply an ice pack on top of the compress to keep it cold longer.

If this technique is applied quickly, immediately following the burn, blisters can often be avoided entirely, and the healing process will take place much faster.

Essential oils are diluted in vegetable oil primarily when the purpose of use is connected with lengthy and thorough massage of the affected area. In an acute, 'hot energy' case, massage is not the relevant response. The quickest and best answer is the hydro-aromatic compress, left on the area and renewed when the 'hotness' is felt again.

Essential oils are absorbed into the organism faster when in a water suspension than when in a dilution of vegetable carrier oil. Absorption—in both cases—is accelerated by heat and slowed down by cold. But the absorption rate in the case of a cold compress on a burn/inflammation actually proceeds fairly quickly because 1) the essential oils are suspended in water rather diluted in vegetable oil, and 2) there is considerable local hot energy from the burn, that actually warms the compress over time. This local heat will not stop immediately. Under the aromatic compress, some heat will initially be drawn out as the cold compress is applied, but the underlying hot energy from the inflammation will progressively recur, and the essential oils will be absorbed little by little into the tissues of the body in a natural process.

In the single essential oil kit I have designed, there are four "cooling" essential oils. Peppermint is the strongest one, but lavender, *Eucalyptus radiata* and geranium also have cooling tendencies. Geranium, in particular, is helpful when edema (an accumulation of fluid) accompanies the hotness, which is often the case with acute inflammation.

In energy medicine, we talk of cold and hot energy, but also dry and humid energy, and these can be paired together. You have probably heard of the yin and the yang. The yin is marked by cold and dry energy, while the yang is characterized by hot and humid energy. We see these pairs in the climates of the earth: at the poles the weather is cold and dry; at the equator it is hot and humid. Similarly, the human body can withstand cold temperatures better as long as it remains dry; and it withstands heat better as long as it can perspire, creating wetness, causing evaporation and cooling.

The fundamental problem in natural medicine is to understand what the body wants to do and to help it in its defense reaction. This means we should not brutally stop the body's reaction, unless in extreme, life threatening cases, but try to gently support its action and keep it under intelligent control. Sometimes the body tends to overreact and when this happens, there can be negative consequences.

I consider many allopathic treatments, in particular the use of corticoids, to be "coercive" on the body, a kind of brutal blockage of all the body's natural reactions, an artificial punishment that does not really serve the natural, self-healing process of the organism. It is possible to use essential oils in a way that is allopathic—blocking rather than complementing the body's natural responses. We have seen well-meaning health practitioners attempt this, but we are convinced that this type of approach—fighting with the body rather than complementing its efforts—is not consistent with the spirit of essential oils.

Natural medicine, by contrast, seeks to enhance the natural processes. This is what I call "life helping life." If we learn how to integrate the energy medicine approach with the use of essential oils, we can become both 'health engineers,' working very precisely and carefully to achieve just the right balance; and also 'health artists' working with aromatic substances rich in harmonious vibrations, to create complementary and beneficial healing environments to sustain normal, natural processes. I envision the day when even the allopathic community will embrace this more practical and natural approach to healing.

Some patients have asked me if there are any more convenient application alternatives besides vegetable oil dilution or aromatic compresses. In fact, it is possible to use a gel or very light neutral cream as a base in which to include essential oils. These enable the very rapid absorption of aromatic compounds into the body, while eliminating some of the fuss and mess of aromatic compresses. Several companies now offer these neutral bases, which can be used when massage is not required. But I still recommend the aromatic compress for acute or serious inflammation. Natural gels and light creams are better suited for speeding up your daily applications, such as applying essential oils or blends in the morning before going to work.

Respiratory and Digestive Relief

Another major purpose for peppermint essential oil is to support and help the respiratory system. Rose-Marie and I have long taught that there is a vital and necessary connection between the respiratory system and the digestive system. We have found that no permanent improvement can be made in the respiratory function without making improvements at the same time in the digestive system. Peppermint essential oil happens to work in a way that reinforces this primary connection.

A most dramatic illustration of this interdependence can be seen in the case of Abby from Australia. This dramatic healing took place in a very short period of time and spared Abby the pain and misery of sinus surgery. Abby's case is documented fully—in her own words—in my book, *Natural Home Health Care Using Essential Oils.* Suffice it to say here, that in order to achieve a dramatic improvement in Abby's respiratory system, which was chronically congested and infected, we had to make a dramatic change in her eating habits. Improvements in her digestive processes were critical in achieving the improvement in her respiratory system and essential oils supported both changes.

This is an excellent example of the interconnectedness of all systems of the body, and how every system is connected to and dependent on the breathing function. Classical/allopathic medicine does not adequately recognize the interconnectedness of all the body systems. It cannot recognize that excessive mucous in the throat and lungs is a sign of poor elimination. It further does not recognize that there is a connection between the production of excess mucous and the foods that are absorbed through the digestive system! The principle is actually very simple. I tell my patients that what they cough, spit, sneeze and expel through their air passages is more strongly linked to the food they eat than it is to the quality of the air they breathe!

This is not to say that if you are a chain-smoking coal miner you will not evacuate toxic elements from the terrible attack made on your lungs. As long as we confine our discussion to typical, normal life, our experience shows that one cannot obtain a swift and deep healing of a respiratory ailment if we do not supplement our aromatic care with proper corrections in nutrition and diet.

We are seeing an increasing number of very small children with chronic lung congestion/infection. We believe that much of this is arising out of the allopathic prescriptions for respiratory congestion that do not take into effect the importance of other systems of the body, particularly the digestive system. Many of these chronic problems in children seem to be directly related to nutritional faults followed by the over-prescribing of antibiotics and cortisone.

The reason peppermint can help so well in these cases is that it has a purifying effect on both systems. Peppermint is absolutely unique and irreplaceable in this role. I often refer to peppermint essential oil as the "trump card" of aromatherapy, because it can often overcome the effects of years of bad habits, enabling us to relatively quickly nullify or cancel lifestyle effects. In the same way peppermint essential oil quickly relieves pain, it can work wonders both on the digestive and on the respiratory systems. I will go even further and say that the powerful positive effect that peppermint has on the respiratory system is largely *because* of the powerful, positive effect that it has on the digestive system.

A basic principle of natural medicine is that we are much more effective—in the long and the short term—when we work on the cause of the problem rather than just alleviate the symptom. Similarly, we are typically more effective when we work from the inside out rather than from the outside in.

Here is a classic example. Almost everyone has—at one time or another—experienced a completely stuffed nose, where both nostrils seem to be completely stopped. Under such conditions, typical allopathic inhalers are almost useless. Even essential oils cannot work on mucous membranes unless the aromatic compounds can reach them. But there is a way to work from the inside on this problem using peppermint, and I encourage you to try this amazing experiment the next time you have a sinus congestion.

Place a drop of peppermint in a spoonful of natural honey. Then place a tsp. of this essential oil/honey mixture on the tongue and suck it slowly between the tongue and the roof of your mouth. You will experience an amazing action on your sinus membranes and in most cases, the effect will be to open the congested passageways of the nose.

This effect is similar to that of a mentholated lozenge. But it is different in that commercially available menthol lozenges are made with synthetic menthol, large amounts of refined sugars and sometimes other ingredients that we cannot recommend. Refined sugar itself can be a primary cause of excess mucous, and it also inhibits normal mineral metabolization, essential to healthy mucous membranes.

When we use a natural essential oil, we are using natural menthol plus many other aromatic compounds that work in synergy with the menthol. Natural honey is a living product, compared to refined sugars, which are completely dead, and we are not adding any artificial flavors, colors or preservatives. So it is much better for your health and probably less expensive to give this natural treatment to yourself.

Once you begin to see that the primary motive behind commercial production is financial profit rather than concern for health—and this applies to the pharmaceutical companies—you will have a much greater incentive to take personal responsibility for your health and to treat yourself with ingredients you know are pure and natural.

When little Abby came in for her intensive treatments over a two-week period, I had her breathe a special aromatic aerosol to help treat her very serious sinus condition. But we began each session by having her suck on some peppermint aromatic honey just to get the vapors into her sinuses so they would unblock long enough to receive the aerosol treatment.

This example demonstrates that peppermint essential oil works on respiratory congestion in two important ways:

1) When the peppermint honey is held in the mouth, peppermint vapors go up the back of the throat to the sinuses, helping to unblock the mucous membranes and allowing air to pass.This is the swift, direct action.
2) Then, because the peppermint honey is eventually swallowed, entering the alimentary canal, the peppermint essential oil will exert a strong purifying action inside the digestive system itself, contributing to a deeper, longer-lasting remedy.

The more you understand the natural processes involved in healing the body, the more motivated you will be to use them. That is why Rose-Marie and I, in our training, try to do more than just tell you what essential oils to use for what problems. We want you to understand how the body processes and the essential oil effects interrelate.

The above approach is completely different from allopathic nasal sprays that contain synthetic vasoconstrictors! Most people who use these devices find that they work for a short time, but then their nasal cavities clog up again, sometimes worse than before. This can start a vicious cycle. I strongly advise you to avoid falling into this dependency trap! The apparent easiness of getting quick results this way is a decoy that may imprison you in a situation that can have very serious consequences.

I once treated a patient who had begun using this allopathic spray for a simple cold. By the time he came to me he had been using these sprays for over 10 years, unable to forsake its use without getting completely congested! These situations are the result of trying to cheat nature and natural processes. It took several months of intensive aromatic and natural care to get this patient back to normal nasal function.

Is there any chance that the same addiction might occur with peppermint essential oil? The answer to this question is emphatically No!, but it raises some important issues that you should understand about holistic medicine vs. allopathic medicine.

I will use the example of a patient named Richard who visited his doctor complaining about chronic nasal and sinus congestion. I will try to illustrate the perceptions of the allopathic doctor treating him vs. the holistic approach.

In the doctors' office, Richard is not seen as Richard, a human being with a past, present and future. He is perceived as a case of nasal congestion. Modern medicine cuts the body into convenient little pieces, figuratively speaking. The Ear-Nose-Throat specialist considered a slice of Richard just a few inches long, from his forehead to the bottom of his lower lip. Nothing above that, nothing below it. And then he endeavored to make Richard's case fit into the 'automatic allopathic response box.' In short, he tried to find a way to justify a quick prescription of antibiotics and/or anti-inflammatories.

Richard did not have to answer any questions about his recent dietary habits, his lifestyle, his emotional state, or any unusual exposure to toxins. His problem was considered in a completely isolated way, disconnected from effects that might have been created by other body systems and organs.

In my opinion, there is little hope for improvement with such a limited approach. Allopathic prescriptions may alleviate the discomfort of some symptoms for a while, but the underlying problem will still be there, and will continue to recur, until the specialist reaches a point where he recommends expensive and painful surgery, which even then by itself does not always solve the problem.

When Richard turns to aromatic/naturopathic methods, he receives a much different program that takes into account many lifestyle factors, including diet, hygiene and emotional stress. Based on detailed background information, Richard receives a comprehensive program involving multiple essential oils and several application methods, plus diet and lifestyle recommendations that work in synergy to eliminate the underlying problem, not just the symptoms. He receives treatment on his neck, back, face, ears and reflex points of the feet, all of which work together to improve his condition. His doctor also trains Richard in how to use essential oils at home between sessions.

You can see that in this second option we have reached a health care approach that is utterly unlike the traditional, allopathic approach. This is how I define holistic medicine. It is my philosophy of how medicine should be practiced. It will come about as doctors continue to place a higher priority on their healing skills than they do on their social and financial standing in the community. Recent statistics from the US show that the average length of time spent by a doctor face-to-face with a patient during an appointment is typically less than 5 minutes! Holistic medicine as I define it cannot be practiced this way.

Holistic medicine opens a pathway that patients can follow as far as they are willing to go, leading to greater and greater health—no longer fighting disease, but embracing health. Integrated aromatic medicine, as I define it, involves using all the natural, holistic medical techniques we know, integrated with essential oil applications and special equipment for effectively administering those essential oils. I believe in this approach to medicine so strongly that I have committed my life to training those who are willing to spread this new and more efficacious style of healing. Someday I hope to see aromatic centers available to the general public. You who are reading this handbook may play an instrumental role in bringing about this new dimension of health freedom.

This approach to health is consistent with the instruction in the New Testament and also found in other religions, that the body is a temple for housing the spirit. A temple is a sacred place, deserving our highest devotions. It is not a place that we would treat lightly or allow to become filthy and foul smelling due to neglect and disrespect. Similarly, our bodies should be treated with care and respect, kept clean and pure from the pollutions of our day.

In no way do I mean to imply that purifying and caring for one's body is in itself sufficient to make one a saint. There are many dimensions of the human soul, and I believe the Creator intended for us to develop all of them. Some of us spend our lives working only on our bodies, making them strong and shapely, but forget the spiritual dimension. Conversely, there are those of us who dedicate our lives to becoming spiritually enlightened but forget—or sometimes intentionally ignore—the development and maintenance of our marvelous physical gift. I am convinced that our bodies are as much a part of our stewardship as our spirits are, with the ideal condition being a pure and strong spirit inside a healthy and clean body.

Essential oils are clearly and scientifically proven to have marvelous beneficial effects on the physical body. I will not elaborate on that here, but I do have strong feelings that essential oils can also assist in strengthening our minds and our spirits, if used properly. Let me simply reaffirm that of all the essential oils, peppermint has a very high purification potential. Peppermint essential oil can be a 'balm of Gilead' that takes away sorrow and discomfort, while it brings a wonderful clarity of thought.

Other Uses

Peppermint essential oil has been found to be effective in relieving nausea, particularly when caused by motion sickness. Simply taking some deep breaths of peppermint essential oil is often sufficient to stop the nausea sensation. For stronger treatment in adults, you can place a trace of peppermint essential oil on the tongue. For very young children I suggest using lemon essence instead of peppermint essential oil. Under the age of 2 years there is a classical contraindication used by pharmacists: products containing menthol should not be used, particularly near the throat or near the nose, because of a risk of inducing a spasm in the larynx.

Peppermint essential oil can help in the case of hiccups. Apply a trace on the back on each side of the cervical column, at the level of the fifth cervical vertebra.

Not directly health related, but nonetheless very practical applications of peppermint essential oil include air freshening by putting a drop or two at the outlet filter of a vacuum cleaner, and also as an insect repellent. Most insects dislike peppermint. Disperse 10 drops of peppermint essential oil in 1 cup of water in a spray bottle. Shake vigorously and then spray into areas where the insects are likely to invade.

Peppermint can also be used as a flavor enhancer. Its fresh and stimulating influence can be a delicious part of many fruit juices, adding one drop to a glass. It also adds wonderful flavor to sorbets.

You should keep in mind that peppermint is considered a stimulating essential oil, meaning it can prevent you from relaxing and sleeping at bedtime. Avoid using it in the evening, if possible. On the other hand, if sinus congestion is keeping you up at night anyway, you have nothing to lose by using the peppermint to bring relief.

Summary

This chapter on peppermint has been somewhat long because of many introductory essential oil concepts we have presented. So let me summarize now, some key points on using this special substance.

1. Peppermint essential oil is very effective in reducing and eliminating pain from trauma (bumps and bruises). One or two drops gently massaged on the affected area will usually do the job. Further healing can be achieved with aromatic compresses and other essential oils.

2. Peppermint essential oil has a very strong purifying and unblocking effect on the whole digestive system, from stomach to bowel; it also works on the liver and on the pancreas. Because of this it is a kind of elementary healing agent. No other essential oil can replace pep-

permint! By working so strongly and effectively on the digestive system, helping to limit the formation and accumulation of mucous, peppermint vitalizes the whole body. The system that benefits most from this purifying and unblocking effect is the respiratory system. We can unblock nasal congestion by putting peppermint honey on the tongue. Deeper effects in the upper respiratory system can be achieved through herbal peppermint tea made with peppermint essential oil and by regularly inhaling the peppermint aroma from a tissue.

3. Peppermint can be effective in bringing relief to headaches. At home the most effective application method is an aromatic compress, but 'on the run' peppermint essential oil can be applied neat in trace amounts on the temples and forehead (taking extra care to be certain no essential oil traces get into the eyes).

4. Peppermint is a 'cooling' essential oil, but should not be placed neat on a burn/inflammation because its high concentration will bring too much energy to the area and ultimately add to the inflammation. A more effective option is to dilute it in water (with a drop or two of lavender essential oil) and use it in an aromatic compress. If this is not convenient, apply the essential oils mixed in a neutral gel or light cream base.

5. Peppermint can help with nausea from motion sickness and with hic cups. It can also be used as an air freshener and an insect repellent.

6. Peppermint is a 'stimulating' essential oil. It is advisable to use small amounts in any application, and it is not advisable to use in the evening or at bedtime, as it may cause insomnia.

Chapter 6: Eucalyptus *(Eucalyptus radiata)*

There are hundreds of different species in the genus Eucalyptus. The native country for most eucalyptus varieties is Australia, but some varieties have been successfully planted and cultivated all over the world. One which we see often is Eucalyptus globulus. Many ask if there is any big difference between this species and the radiata species. In fact, there are important differences that make the radiata variety better suited for essential oil therapy in the context of use by lay people.

The globulus species is indeed a magnificent tree, but when you distill its leaves, you obtain a less-refined essential oil, one that I consider potentially unsafe. I am not saying it is poison in any way. The problem is that it contains a small amount of a compound that can trigger a coughing reaction when inhaled. For an essential oil that is mainly used to help the respiratory system, this is not an ideal situation! In order to get rid of this irritating compound called 'isovaleraldehyde,' the raw essential oil is redistilled, in the same way that crude oil is submitted to fractionated distillation in the chemical industry. This redistilled or 'rectified' Eucalyptus globulus essential oil is what is typically found in stores, and it usually does not come from Australia, but from China. China is a world leader in the production of eucalyptus essential oil, exporting many tons of it every year. This product is not dangerous or harmful, but it is what I would consider an industrial product. It is sold as a raw material that other industries use in various commercial products to give them a fresh aroma.

This type of essential oil is better suited to what I call "recreational fragrancing" than it is to true aromatherapy. Particularly in the US, aggressive marketing campaigns have given the word aromatherapy a very different meaning than it has in France. In France we still view it as a medical term. In the US it seems anything with a nice odor is called aromatherapy, regardless of what may have created that odor. Many so-called 'aromatherapy' products are not at all beneficial from a true therapy standpoint. That is why I think we need a term like "recreational fragrancing"—to separate natural, plant-derived essential oil products that can help the body, from the cheap, sweet-smelling odors that come from test tubes and chemical mixing vats.

Looking at the single oils in my kit geographically, there are four continents represented, two from each continent. Australia supplies *Eucalyptus radiata* and Tea tree. Peppermint and balsam fir come from North America. Lavender and lemon come from countries in Europe, and Africa is represented by tropical basil and geranium.

It is very important in considering essential oils, to distinguish between those produced on an industrial scale and those produced for medical aromatherapy. There are major differences in how the plants are grown, harvested, distilled and distributed. Essential oils—when produced very carefully (almost always on a limited scale) contain hundreds of complex organic compounds. Some are found in small quantities, but yet in just the right amount to create healing synergy. When essential oils are produced hastily or harshly, only for the sake of an aroma or a taste, many of the very beneficial aromatic compounds are completely lost, rendering the essential oil useless for therapy.

This difference in quality also carries a price tag. High quality essential oils always cost a lot more than industrial essential oils. Generally speaking, if a bottle of essential oil in a store seems quite inexpensive, then it is probably an industrial grade essential oil and often will not provide any of the beneficial results I speak of in this book. I have a motto, which I often repeat, that "I would rather have one drop of genuine, high quality essential oil than a whole drum of junk product." In the arena of aromatic medicine, junk product has no role to play at all. We must have the highest quality essential oils available in order to enjoy health benefits from them. That is why I personally selected and tested the oils in my kits. I know the distillers first hand, and I know the essential oils they produce are therapeutic grade, not industrial grade.

This issue of quality is one which I have come to understand much better in the last 10 years. It comes into real focus in determining the quantity of essential oil needed for a given application. I went through a major shift in thinking on this subject several years ago.

When you have a lab and work with large quantities of essential oils, it's easy to assume that large amounts of essential oil will do a better job for a health problem than small amounts will. I confess that in my early years I advocated the use of fairly large amounts of essential oils, especially during intensive aromatic care. These large amounts of oil were applied primarily through topical (skin) application. We got generally good results from this quantitative approach, which encouraged us to continue with it.

The paradigm shift on quantity began for me one day in a discussion with Robert Tisserand, a very well known English aromatherapist and author of many books. He said that in his experience and in some studies, essential oils seemed to work well either in large amounts or in quite small ones, and that there was relatively poor response for quantities between these two extremes. This got me to thinking about how I was getting results. My approach was essentially a 'shotgun' approach, applying so much essential oil over so much area, that I was bound to hit some of the important spots.

But I began to realize, through my study of energy medicine, Chinese meridians and the body's reflex points, that essential oils could be used in a 'rifle shot' manner, by using much smaller quantities applied directly on key reflex points on the body. I also found that tiny amounts of very high quality essential oil can have profound effects when applied at just the right point. Low-grade essential oils do not bring such results

The key ingredient is to identify which points on the body are the key receptor points, where topical applications of small amounts of essential oils will have the greatest effect. By finding these sites and using them, significant results can be achieved with just a few drops. In selecting these points on the body, we always consider the acupuncture meridians of Chinese medicine. Additionally, we use a lot of the reflex points from reflexology. The Chinese pathways and the reflexology points do not always correspond with each other, but both approaches are helpful in identifying sites that will work. We find them all over the body, on the hands, face, ears, skull and particularly the feet.

Of particular importance are the points that influence the various organs. These are located along the spine, from the nape of the neck to the sacrum.

Eucalyptus radiata's primary function is to help all the parts of the respiratory system. In cases of infection, its best role is in counteracting viruses rather than bacteria (which is more the role of Tea tree, ***Melaleuca alternifolia***). Using my 'old' methods—before I began to appreciate the effectiveness of using key reflex points—I might have applied 5 ml on my chest and another 5 ml on my back. I would use an entire 10 ml bottle in one application! You can appreciate the magnitude of change in my thinking. When I changed my approach, I used only several drops of Eucalyptus, applied in very specific spots. . . .and the results were just as good. Here again, high quality essential oil is mandatory. If you do not have essential oils that you know are therapeutic grade, then you should use another therapy. My role is to help you in providing the highest quality essential oils and also to instruct you on the application locations—the reflex points—that will bring the best results.

So let me begin to identify where the 'energy' points are for applying eucalyptus. In most cases, eucalyptus should be used neat for topical applications. (This is not the case, however, for my respiratory blend, which is much more complex and is quite powerful. In most cases, my blends should be used in a diluted form.)

Whenever applying eucalyptus, whether in a static application of drops or a dynamic application involving body contacts, it is always recommended that you take deep breaths, to bring aromatic molecules into the respiratory system.

If you look at a diagram showing the reflex points on the feet, you will see that the tips of the toes represent the sinuses. By symmetry, the tips of the fingers also are reflex points for the sinuses. So my first exercise with eucalyptus, intended to help clear and stimulate the sinuses, involves the fingertips. It may seem a little unusual at first, but we have had consistently good results with this simple exercise.

Apply a trace of the eucalyptus to the tip of each finger, right at the center of the top of the finger, where the nail edge and the skin meet. Do this using the edge of a dropper or pipette, so that you should only need 2-3 drops to cover all ten fingers. If we just left the essential oil on the fingertips at this point, it would be a static application, and it is helpful, even if we do nothing else. We can make it a dynamic application and activate a greater energy flow by tapping the five fingertips of the left hand against the corresponding fingertips of the right hand very rapidly. Do this 50 to 100 times in 15-20 seconds. Do this exercise holding the fingertips just under your nose, enabling you to breathe deeply the eucalyptus aroma. This then becomes a two-step application, with the eucalyptus stimulating the reflex points in the fingers, which connect to the sinuses, and the eucalyptus molecules reaching the sinus walls directly through breathing. You should find that this exercise creates clearing in the sinuses and increases the depth of your breathing, resulting in better oxygenation.

The above exercise can also be performed on the tips of the toes, tapping each toe with the middle finger of the corresponding hand.

Another beneficial application site is at the reflex point for the lungs that is located on the external ear. This point is located in the lower part of the cartilage area of the ear. A trace of Eucalyptus radiata is picked up with the little finger and applied to the outer side of the ear on this point. A second trace is then applied to the corresponding area on the opposite side of the ear. This application should be done on both ears.

Other locations for stimulating the lungs can be found on the hands and on the feet. On the feet, the site is the area under the toes. A drop is applied across the area under all five toes and then the area is massaged with the thumb. Similarly on the hands, the area to stimulate is the upper palm of the hand, just below the base of the fingers. Apply a drop on the left hand and cover this area with the corresponding area of the palm of the right hand and rub the palms together to activate the penetration of the essential oil.

There are additional points that correspond with the Chinese meridians. These are on the lung meridian and the bladder meridian, both left and right sides. The lung meridian starts on the chest, on the pectorals major muscle, two fingerwidths under the clavicle at the level of its external third part. Put a drop of Eucalyptus radiata on the right middle finger and apply it to the left side, massaging five times in an upward direction. The same is done with the left middle finger on the right side.

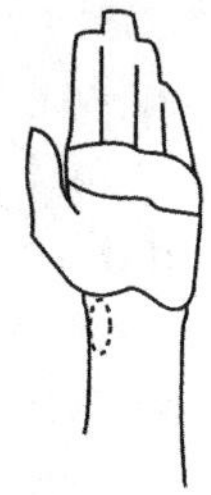

On the wrists, simply put a drop on your left wrist at the point where you would normally take your pulse. Then place the same point on the right wrist over the left wrist and turn the wrists on each other clockwise for a few seconds.

The last meridian point for the lungs is the bladder meridian. Chinese medicine teaches that we can treat what is up by what is down; what is left by what is right; what is on the front by what is on the back, and vice versa. Whenever an anterior organ is not functioning well, it is important to reharmonize its function by working on its posterior reflex point.

Again, remember I am not talking about serious or life-threatening complications here. I am assuming that whenever necessary, a health professional will be consulted to properly diagnose and treat severe problems. Aromatic treatments can almost always be made in conjunction with medical treatment, and they usually help speed the healing process and strengthen the action of regular medical treatment.

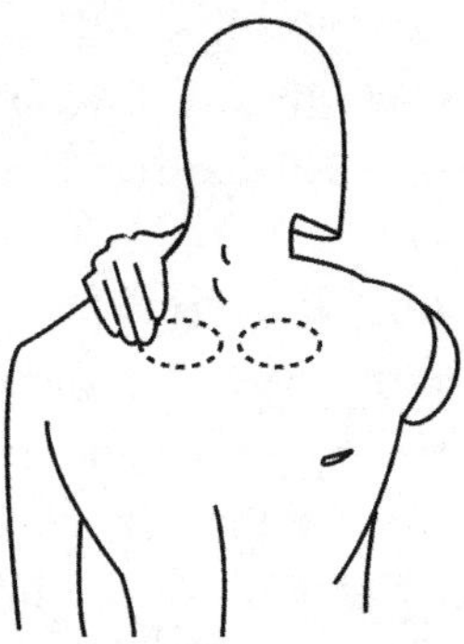

The point of the bladder meridian that controls the lungs is located approximately one inch on either side of the spine, at the level of the space between the third and fourth thoracic vertebrae. This might sound complicated, but it is actually quite easy to locate. If you are working on someone else's back, have them bend their head forward as far as they can. The most prominent projection along the upper spine is the first thoracic vertebrae. It is as if the Creator wanted all of us to be able to locate it easily. Put your finger on the project and move it down slowly, first to the space between the first and second thoracic vertebrae, then to the space between the second and third thoracic vertebrae. Go one more step to the space between the third and fourth thoracic vertebrae. The energy spots we are seeking are one inch on either side of this point on the spine. Apply 1-2 drops to each of these points and massage in a clockwise motion.

With practice this application can be self-administered. Place a drop of eucalyptus on your right middle finger and reach it over your left shoulder. If you are reasonably limber, your left middle finger will reach almost exactly to the bladder meridian lung spot on your left side. The right middle finger in turn can reach to the left side. After applying the essential oil, massage a few seconds turning a clockwise circle.

I believe this simple technique of applying eucalyptus to the bladder meridian is the most noticeably effective one for helping the lungs and harmonizing the breathing function. It is wise to begin with this application, because it will facilitate and enhance the results of the other application techniques.

There is one more classical point, which belongs to the large intestine meridian that I will mention. It is located at the summit of the angle made by the first and second metacarpal bones of the thumb and the forefinger (see diagram). Apply one drop to this point and massage in clockwise motion.

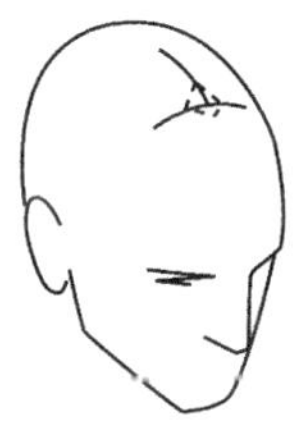

Additionally there are two more spots that eucalyptus can stimulate well. One is at the sides of the nose. This is the ending of the large intestine meridian. Whenever applying essential oil to the face, use only tiny trace amounts. Apply the trace to the outside of each nostril. The final point is at the very top of the skull, along the seam line, where you would find the soft part on a baby's skull. This application can be quite helpful in decongesting stuffed sinuses and a blocked nose, when done in conjunction with the peppermint-drop-in-a-spoonful-of-honey application described earlier.

Eucalyptus radiata, like peppermint, can be taken internally in trace amounts. A drop in orange or apple juice is quite nice. Like peppermint, it can be taken in some honey. When you want to take full advantage of the energy points applications, it is advisable to drink a drop of eucalyptus radiata in a beverage before starting the bodywork. Some people notice a definite increase in the effect of the skin applications when they do this.

Again, I emphasize that eucalyptus's great role in the human body is helping the respiratory system, including the sinuses and even the ears. A recent example demonstrates this. On our last trip to the US in 1999, we visited with some of our friends in Utah. While we were there, their six-year old son, Jackson, was starting a respiratory infection that had congested his nasal cavities and was creating a painful earache. He had a slight fever. The typical response in this situation is to call the doctor, and you know what the almost-reflex response will be: antibiotics. I don't mean to imply that you should not call the doctor, especially if there is room for doubt as to what the infection is all about. A medical examination and diagnosis is of critical importance.

In this particular case, however, we had a large vial of eucalyptus radiata with us and we decided to use this single essential oil on Jackson. I began by massaging his feet with *Eucalyptus radiata* diluted in virgin olive oil. To address the earache, I put some neat essential oil on the reflex point of the ear, located under the fourth toe on each foot. We then gently massaged some diluted eucalyptus on the child's thorax, front and back, on the neck and around the ears. Finally, we prepared compresses soaked with *Eucalyptus radiata* dispersed in cold water, as described in the peppermint chapter. These were wrapped around both wrists and both ankles and covered with a cling film.

Within 30 minutes, the child was clearly improved. The fever was lower, and the earache pain was tapering off. The family followed our instructions after this initial treatment and within a few days the child was symptom free. With essential oil applications, it is very important to spend extra time at the beginning of the treatment, repeating applications fairly frequently—sometimes as often as three times per hour—until the problem is under control. Then the frequency of treatment can be reduced as improvement progresses.

In cases of fever it is well to remember that fever is a means of the body to eliminate an infection. Artificially stopping the fever symptoms, such as with aspirin and Tylenol, can be potentially dangerous. As explained before, in natural medicine, we try to act in a way that respects what the body is trying to do. *Eucalyptus radiata*, which is a cool essential oil because of its high content of eucalyptole or 1,8 cineole, will help control a fever, but not in a brutal or artificial way. With infants, if the fever really gets too high, it is often safer to give them a bath in water that is four degrees cooler than the fever. We also use the water compresses with *Eucalyptus radiata* dispersed in cold water.

There are two old aromatic remedies we use in Europe, involving onions. The first is used when a child's fever is too high and must be tempered. Several fresh onions are pureed in a blender. This puree is placed on a cling film and wrapped around the foot and ankle of the feverish child at bedtime. This onion poultice is kept on all night. The next morning, the child is often dramatically improved. The poultice is removed and the onions appear 'cooked' from the heat absorbed from the child's body during the night.

The second onion remedy is for earaches. By grating an onion and squeezing it, you can extract a small amount of onion 'juice.' A few drops of this juice are blended with a teaspoon of virgin olive oil. Place a drop of this oil warmed to body temperature (check by touching a drop on your lips) at the entrance to the ear by using a cotton swab, then cover the entrance to the ear with a piece of cotton. This has worked very well with our own children, and we have recommended it successfully to dozens of our patients.

You might not at first think of these remedies as being 'aromatic' in nature, because there are no essential oils involved. However, onions, as well as garlic, are very rich in aromatic compounds. There is such a thing as essential oil of onion and garlic, but these are so concentrated in sulfur compounds that they are very unpleasant! It is much simpler—and less expensive—to turn to the natural vegetable.

We are often asked about the safety issues of treating infants with essential oils. It is true that young children are more sensitive to essential oils because they are so concentrated, but if used carefully, they can bring wonderful results for infants, particularly with common respiratory infections. I will relate two examples.

One very young male patient was quite congested, and having a hard time sleeping because of it. He was afraid to take the medicine his doctor had supplied and his parents were concerned about how they could treat it. I simply suspended a small diffuser above the boy's crib and slowly diffused a mixture of *Eucalyptus radiata* and tea tree. As the little boy inhaled these vapors, he was able to relax and soon went to sleep. All night, as he breathed, the aromatic vapors entered his respiratory system, and in the morning when he awoke his condition had improved for the first time.

In another recent case, a mother called me about her five-month-old son. Even though she had breast fed him, he had come down with some kind of an infection. Their doctor had been consulted, and he diagnosed a bronchial infection and congestion in the left ear. His prescription was, as you would expect, antibiotics. The mother and father were both very involved in natural medicine, and reluctant to give antibiotics to such a small child, they called me. I told her to make a blend of three essential oils, eucalyptus radiata, tea tree and lavender, and to apply two drops of this blend neat on the sole of each foot. I further recommended that she dilute some of this blend in olive oil and use it to massage the baby's thorax and behind his ears. She repeated this procedure four times per hours the first few hours, in order to get the problem under control. As the baby improved, the frequency was reduced to three times per hour then twice and finally once per hour. Within three days, the baby was symptom free.

Having helped hundreds of mothers win similar victories with their babies, I am convinced that the aromatic way has no equivalent in allopathic medicine. You will probably be skeptical until you see the results, and we have seen wonderful results over and over again. Using natural medicine is not necessarily an easy path! There is a lot more to it than asking a child to swallow a spoonful of the latest antibiotic syrup. It usually involves more work, such as repeatedly massaging and wrapping and comforting a child. But it is exciting to see that the end results are complete healing, and that patients have learned ways to help themselves and approach health problems with more confidence.

Rose Marie and I try to 'walk our talk' as they say. In our own family, none of our three children has ever taken an antibiotic. Yes, they did experience the usual infections, though less than most children because we were very careful with their nutrition. We only used aromatherapy, homeopathy and general natural medicine and it always worked.

Before I conclude this chapter I want to remind you to consider with reverence the miracle of essential oils. Whenever you open a vial of essential oil and smell its rich aroma, I hope you will do it with a feeling of immense respect toward the amazing work of nature that produced this substance. Let your feelings of gratitude go out to all the people who contributed to make these essential oils available to you.

You are part of a human network that is growing faster every day. You are part of the human family that has learned what an amazing natural gift our Creator has given to us to help us take care of our bodies and our spirits.

Remember that there are vibrations in and around all of us, and the thankful, respectful thoughts you have as you use essential oils will not only help you but those around you as you seek to comfort and help them. You can be part of an increasing collective vibration around aromatic plants and essential oils.

Chapter 7: Tea Tree *(Melaleuca alternifolia)*

The third essential oil in our first group, like eucalyptus, comes from Australia. It is distilled from a tree commonly known as the tea tree, but is also becoming recognized by its Latin name, *Melaleuca alternifolia.* Just as eucalyptus is our first choice for dealing with viral infections in the respiratory system, so tea tree is our first choice for dealing with bacterial infections not only in the respiratory area, but also in all systems of the body. I am tempted to call *Melaleuca alternifolia* the natural antibiotic, but that would not be semantically correct.

A Natural Probiotic

You see, the term antibiotic literally means "opposed to life" (anti = against + biotic = pertaining to life). It is supposed to suggest opposition to the life of the offending bacteria, but sadly, it is also opposed to the life of helpful bacteria as well. Herein lies an enormous difference between essential oils and antibiotics.

A more appropriate term for melaleuca would be probiotic or eubiotic, meaning "in favor of, or in support of life." In this case it would refer to the life of the organism being attacked by unfriendly bacteria.

We sometimes mistakenly assume that it is a good thing to eliminate ALL bacteria in our systems. But this is entirely incorrect. The truth is that many microorganisms, including bacteria, are absolutely essential to life in general and human body function in particular. Only a small percentage is harmful. Many allopathic doctors seem to be unaware of the importance of what we call "terrain," meaning the conditions that must be present for bacteria to breed and multiply. Our amazing immune system is equipped to deal with most microbes that are harmful. We all know that when there is a "bug in the air," some people get sick, but others do not. The allopathic approach to disease involves heavy and sometimes indiscriminant use of antibiotics, which indiscriminately kills all internal bacteria, even the vital ones. This has made us vulnerable to many other dreadful degenerative diseases. Lately we have been repeatedly told of many new disease strains that are completely resistant to all but the very strongest antibiotics.

I will give you some fascinating history, but before I do, I want to make a very important distinction between the antibacterial activity of antibiotics and that of essential oils, particularly melaleuca. *The point is this: while antibiotics kill indiscriminately, essential oils—being a special product of life—seem to have an amazing ability to discern which bacteria are life-promoting and which are destructive. And they kill only the destructive strains!* Why this happens is too complex for scientists to explain, so again we allow nature to be complex so we can be simple. Somehow the Creator has endowed essential oils with some form of intelligence that allows them to discriminate for our benefit, neutralizing only the strains and locations that are problematic. As amazing as this fact is, very few health professionals are aware of it.

Now let me give you some history. In 1928, as Sir Alexander Fleming was discovering penicillin in England, René-Maurice Gattefossé and others were laying the foundation of scientific and medical aromatherapy in Lyon, France—only two hours drive from our home. Interestingly, on the other side of the world, at nearly the same time, Australian researchers were performing high level experiments that proved the efficacy of essential oils, especially *Melaleuca alternifolia*, in fighting bacterial infections. The sudden and overwhelming acceptance of antibiotics led to their industrial production in the early 1940's, particularly in the US. This cast a long shadow over the work of French and Australian researchers using essential oils to fight infection. Thankfully, this did not eliminate their work, but it proceeded relatively unnoticed by researchers in North America.

I believe it was no accident that I was born just a few months after Gattefossé died. My education involved me in both allopathic as well as natural medicine, climaxed by my meeting and collaborating with biochemist Pierre Franchomme. Our book, *L'aromathérapie exactemen*t gave birth to the concept of modern aromatic medicine. Then, through marvelous circumstances, I was able to take my family to Australia for two years, solidifying the French/Australian research connection on essential oils used as medicines. I then returned to France with all the benefits of having practiced medical aromatherapy in a country that is close to France from an aromatic point of view.

Most doctors are beginning to see that we have taken antibiotics too far. In our hellish race to make stronger and stronger medicines that kill life, we are creating horrific diseases for which we have no remedy. We must learn to work with our bodies, not against them, and essential oils provide that path.

Melaleuca alternifolia has great potential as an antibacterial agent, but it is different from conventional antibiotics in that it attacks only destructive bacteria. It was created from life to help life. It knows what to do.

The Lick Trick—An Aromatic Mouth "Wash"
Here is an interesting experiment that everyone should try. Remove the dropper from the vial of tea tree essential oil and brush a trace of it on the back of your hand. Then lick it off with your tongue. Let the aromatic trace mix thoroughly with your saliva and keep it in your mouth.

Let me tell you what has happened. You have just changed your saliva into powerful aromatic medicine! It is not a medicine that will have any side effects. It is not a medicine that will annihilate all microscopic life in your body. It is not a medicine that will confuse your immune system and create autoimmune reactions like some antibiotics do. This is a medicine that was conceived by the Creator in the oldest and finest of laboratories. It is a medicine so finely tuned that it will support friendly bacteria while it eliminates harmful bacteria. Besides this direct action, it stimulates the human immune system to help you stay free of disease.

Using Avogadro's number, I have estimated that there are about 4,000,000,000,000,000,000 molecules of the most active component of tea tree contained in the trace you licked off the back of your hand. That component is known as terpineol-4. Of course, this molecule is accompanied by hundreds of other identified synergistic molecules. The total population of aromatic molecules in your mouth is probably 3 times this amount with a large variety of aromatic compounds! This represents a sizeable assembly of life-giving molecules.

By now the saliva in your mouth has mixed fully with the trace of tea tree oil. Allow it to move to the back of your throat, coating the pharynx and the amygdals. If you happen to have a sore throat, you will feel its action on the throat lining immediately. If your infection is caused by a virus, you need not worry. Unlike antibiotics, which have little or no effect on viruses, tea tree oil has been shown to be antibacterial, antiviral, and antifungal! After coating the back of your mouth for a few seconds, you can swallow your saliva, knowing that the miracle molecules of tea tree oil will continue to have beneficial impact in your digestive tract. In fact, here is where they really do a great service, because *illness usually stems from a weak immune system and congestive toxemia, which are both invariably tied to problems in the digestive tract, particularly the intestines.*

The aroma and taste of tea tree oil are not particularly exciting, but they are not unpleasant either. Although tea tree oil can create a highly acidic pH in the mouth—an environment not friendly to the growth and multiplication of bacteria—it does not taste as acidic as lemon juice, for example. But once you have experienced first-hand the power of tea tree to relieve and heal a sore throat, you will find the taste and aroma very reasonable!

I remember the case of the son of a patient of ours, an 18-year old boy who was very reluctant to try a trace of tea tree essential oil in his mouth. When he got a severe sore throat he was curious enough to ask his mother about the strange-flavored liquid he had seen her lick off the back of her hand. He finally agreed to try the lick trick, and he was stunned to find that after doing it three times in three minutes, the pain of his sore throat vanished.

Another colleague had experienced allergy-related bronchitis every spring and fall for many years of his life. He had tried everything, including extremely powerful antibiotics, but nothing seemed to stop the course of this bronchitis infection once he began to feel the dreaded tickle in the back of his throat. When he tried licking a trace of tea tree off the back of his hand, he discovered something that—for the first time—made the tickle go away! He became so comfortable with it that he made it a point to always keep a bottle of tea tree essential oil with him during the spring and fall. He has been able to avoid bronchitis now for nearly four years.

What About Aggressive Oils?

Many ask me why I do not include some of the very powerful essential oils, such as oregano and thyme in my basic kit of single essential oils. The first and foremost reason is safety. I want these essential oils to be taken seriously as safe alternatives to allopathic prescriptions. The strong essential oils are certainly efficient in some cases, but they are not always safe. Oils like oregano, thyme, and lemongrass have the potential to literally burn the skin, if not used properly. Tea tree, on the other hand, is a powerful antibacterial, antiviral, and antifungal medicine that is perfectly safe. With repeated applications, it can be as effective as the stronger essential oils.

Please understand that I do use the strong essential oils in my practice, and in time, you can learn to use them safely. But these essential oils require a thorough knowledge of biochemistry to be used safely. My knowledge of the strong side and the soft side of essential oils enables me to use them in a way that can be precisely adapted to a particular circumstance. This is why the blends I have created are a perfect complement to the single oils. Believe me, with the single oils and blends I have recommended you will have all the power you need to keep yourself healthy.

Aromatherapists sometimes say that one should be guided in choosing the essential oils to use, by what most pleases the sense of smell. There is some truth in this, but it is not a simple rule. Tea tree, for example, is not an essential oil that people are often drawn to by its aroma. However, it is what I consider to be a staple essential oil in terms of keeping your health. When we use essential oils to deal with medical conditions, as we French doctors often do, we often recommend internal/oral prescriptions of essential oils, and the olfactory aspect is not really as important in these applications (as it might be in English-style aromatherapy). If you are giving a relaxing massage, the aroma of the essential or the essential oil blend used plays a major role.

Tea Tree Oil's Great Contribution—Helping the Digestive System

I maintain that the greatest contribution to be made by tea tree oil is in disinfecting the digestive system. As essential oils go, tea tree is really not too bad in taste. Many essential oils have a much sharper and much more unusual flavor.

Tea tree essential oil can be used on the skin and in a diffuser. It is a wonderful first aid antiseptic for minor cuts and scratches. But nature indicates to us that the best way to tap its full healing potential is to take it internally. Tea tree essential oil is the staple essential oil for all my internal prescriptions, whenever there is a need to help make the intestinal system pure and clean. And this type of cleansing is essential for all patients who come to me with chronic problems of any kind, whether respiratory, urinary, digestive, hormonal, skin, joints, or even psychological problems!

The population of microbes that inhabits your digestive system—especially in the colon—is ten times more numerous than all the cells in your body. If this population gets out of balance, and is overrun by harmful bacteria that in turn secrete harmful toxins, these poisons will penetrate to your blood stream and reach every part of your body, including your brain and its sensitive receptors. You can't possibly feel well and be fit if you are filled with these toxins. Moreover, if you have an unhealthy diet, your situation can degrade to the point where the harmful bacteria actually cross the intestinal wall and find a home in another part of your body. This 'other part of your body' is most often the respiratory system.

Any action that tends to purify the digestive system by neutralizing the toxins and the aggressive bacteria will invariably have far-reaching beneficial consequences in the respiratory system AND in other systems. I will give you one example.

A friend developed a serious inflammation in her left eye, which became red and irritated. Anyone in such a case should consult an ophthalmologist, of course. And that's exactly what she did. The eye doctor completed his exam and found a complicated Greek name ending with "-itis" to describe her condition. His prescription was predictable: local and internal cortisone applications. For us who use natural medicine, this is a remedy for a symptom, but will definitely not get to the root of the problem. It is a cover-up, not a treatment. But most allopathic specialists, because of the nature of their training, are unable to tackle health problems at their root. It's just not part of their conceptual framework.

When this friend came to me, I did not focus on her inflamed eye, but instead worked with her to set up a complete health regimen, starting with the digestive system. She received colonic irrigations and was put under a strong purifying internal program with essential oils, using tea tree primarily. This was accompanied by nutritional corrections and reflexology massage. Improvement came very quickly and when she returned to her doctor, he was convinced that it was his cortisone treatment that had done all the work. If we had not used the internal prescription of essential oils and cleansed the digestive system, there would have been no possibility of obtaining such results.

Daily Use of Tea Tree Oil

Is there a way each day to take advantage of the wonderful properties of tea tree essential oil? Yes and it is simple, quick, and easy. Simply put one drop of tea tree oil in a glass of fresh juice. I usually use apple or orange. By consuming tea tree essential oil in juice—or in the form of an herbal tea with honey—it is absorbed directly in the stomach, rather than in the intestines. When taken on its own with no other food, the molecules of tea tree essential oil will be absorbed, circulated throughout the body, and eliminated through the kidneys within 30-60 minutes.

The action of the ingested tea tree oil is enhanced by applying a drop on each of the external kidney areas. The combination of both internal and external application is typically synergistic. If we assume that internal use represents a therapeutic degree of 7 and external application on the kidney a degree of 3, the combination of both is not 7 + 3, but more like 7 x 3.

Cystitis

Consider the situation with cystitis (bladder infection), a common problem with women and sometimes with men. A medical doctor will always prescribe antibiotics for this problem. Again, natural medicine demands that we intervene—in an intelligent and respectful way—to help the body rid itself completely of the infection, without side effects and in a way that strengthens the body's ability to resist future attacks. Intensive aromatic care provides an alternative to antibiotics that can have dramatic effects in a single day.

For the day of intensive treatment, you would prepare one and a half liters of herbal tea. This should be made from the dried leaves of any herbal tea that is helpful to the digestive system, such as raspberry, alfalfa, peppermint, or a combination of these. Do not use English tea or black tea. It must be true herbal tea containing no caffeine. You should drink three cups of tea during the first hour, then two cups every hour thereafter all day. In each cup, include a drop of tea tree essential oil mixed in honey, and also apply another drop on your back behind each kidney. Do not take any dairy products of any kind. If you need to have something to eat, my advice is to eat apples. Make an apple puree in your blender, or prepare stewed apples or unsweetened applesauce. To each cup of puree or unsweetened applesauce, add one or two drops of tea tree essential oil.

After 12 hours, you will have consumed 25 cups of tea, containing 25 drops of tea tree essential oil. Additionally, you will have applied at least 50 drops of tea tree essential oil on the kidney areas. You may have taken additional tea tree oil internally with apples. This process will literally purify and disinfect the bladder and the kidneys. Remember that tea tree will support any beneficial bacteria and will attack the harmful bacteria. At the same time it will stimulate the immune system and the immune cells so the body can do its own repair and correction. After one day of this intensive treatment, most of our patients can feel a dramatic change taking place inside.

Can Essential Oils be Used While Taking Antibiotics?

Many patients ask whether it is appropriate to use tea tree or any other essential oil while taking antibiotics. This is a good question. In my opinion it is highly advisable to use essential oils while taking antibiotics. It is precisely when antibiotics are being taken that essential oils are most indispensable.

One of the common complications of using antibiotics is the development of fungal infections, in particular candidiasis. These can be local or systemic, creating considerable discomfort and greatly impairing the body's normal function. With strong aromatic treatments, fungal infections go away. Antibiotics, of course, are created from fungi, while essential oils are typically antifungal in their action, especially tea tree oil. If essential oils are taken with antibiotics you greatly limit the risk of fungal infection.

Along these lines, I can relate a marvelous case history that illustrates how complementary essential oils can be to antibiotic treatments. Our patient Mireille was seriously hurt in a truck accident. Her thigh was run over by one of the truck's wheels, and she was rushed to the hospital to save her life and her badly injured leg. Her life and leg were saved, but she had a huge scar that created much pain for her. She came to us some years after the accident for help with this pain. In July of 1999 she called me complaining of very serious pain in her knee. Knowing that she still had pieces of metal inside and along her leg bones, I advised her to go immediately to the hospital. The doctors there discovered an infection in her knee and advised that she must take a high dosage of unusually strong antibiotics over a period of at least two years. The emergency treatment was begun in the hospital, and then she was released with her prescription. The surgeon and other specialists who had diagnosed her case were convinced that she would experience serious systemic problems because of the extended intake of heavy antibiotics.

What they did not know was that Mireille would ask to receive, along with her antibiotics, a similarly strong aromatic treatment. I prepared an appropriate blend of essential oils, and she took them internally, two capsules three times per day for a total of six capsules each day. The blend was diluted before being put in the capsules, but still, this dosage put almost 1 ml of the pure essential oil blend in her system daily. Additionally, she applied another essential oil blend externally on a daily basis.

The results of this combined treatment were amazing, particularly to the doctors who handled her case. They were surprised that when she returned for her regular checkups, she was not feeling exhausted, weak, or depressed as almost all other patients following their regimen did. Second, when they decided to check her blood, they were surprised to find it quite normal, not showing the typical signs of a major infection. Puzzled, they decided to perform a very elaborate test through which her white blood cells were made recognizable by a fine radiographic analysis. They discovered to their surprise that the healing process was almost complete in her case, after only six months of treatment. So they stopped the antibiotics! Mireille was persuaded to speak to her doctors about her extracurricular essential oil treatments, and most of them had to admit that medical aromatherapy had performed a remarkable and complementary healing role. She had healed in six months instead of two years and had experienced none of the usual dreaded complications. Even her intestinal flora had remained in good condition.

I am certain the time will come when the medical community will recognize the tremendous benefits of complementing their methods with aromatic medicine. It will come all the earlier because more and more people are beginning to study essential oils and to use them in ways that go far beyond the shallow concept of recreational fragrancing. This is another reason why I am so careful about the issue of safety in using essential oils, so that this wonderful natural science can progress to wide acceptance with the full respect of the medical community.

Some natural health books advocate merely fasting to allow the body to heal itself. This is an extreme approach to natural health care. It assumes that any intervention on the body's own workings other than fasting and rest, is not truly natural and helpful. I have some respect for this position, but it is too pure for the practical needs of most people. Each life has many dimensions and demands—social, family, professional, psychological, religious, etc. To successfully follow a fast-and-do-nothing else approach, I think you would have to live with many fewer demands than is normal and usual. My medical experience tells me we need to deal with all the dimensions of life. We need to find a happy medium somewhere between the extreme approach that leaves everything to nature and the allopathic approach where purely symptomatic interventions are the rule.

Tea tree essential oil is a general-purpose anti-infection essential oil, and you will probably find yourself using it frequently in your microkit. When any kind of cut or opening of the skin takes place, it can be disinfected immediately with a drop of tea tree essential oil.

External application compliments internal application

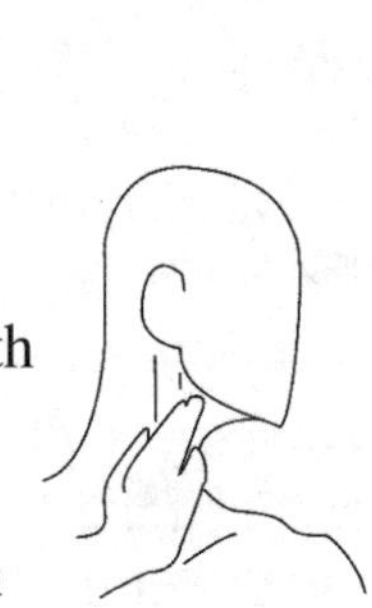

You know about treating sore throats and tonsillitis with aromatic saliva, but you can also help these infections with an external application on the lymph nodes in the throat/neck area. Apply a drop along the lymphatic chain, from the mastoid to the collarbone, going downward. You can also apply a drop under the angle of the inferior maxillary (jaw). This application will activate the production of antibodies by the lymphocytes that reside in the lymph nodes.

Another helpful application in cases of sore throat, tonsillitis, sinusitis is along the nape of the neck. You will recall that I mentioned that when there is a problem in the front part of the body, it has to be tackled from the rear. In this case, the rear is the nape of the neck. It should be carefully massaged in a downward direction, from the occipital bone on the back of the head to the trapezius muscle, on each side. You can use a blend of two drops tea tree essential oil in six drops carrier oil. You can also add two drops of lavender oil to this mixture if you feel there is a lot of muscle tension in the neck.

In some acute cases where there is a high risk of serious infection, external applications of tea tree essential oil must be done in large amounts. This was the case for me when a rusty nail pierced through my shoe and entered the sole of my foot. I described this case in detail in my earlier book, *Natural Home Health Care Using Essential Oils.* Because I felt there was a risk of very serious infection, I made many liberal applications of tea tree essential oil on this wound, both in and around the nail hole and following the lymphatic pathway up to the groin lymphatic node. I used more than 20 ml in the first hour and supported absorption with the use of a hair dryer, set to a very mild heat temperature.

Eye Infections

Many people are surprised to learn that tea tree essential oil can be used to help with eye infections and with toothaches. You know that essential oils should normally kept away from any contact with the eyes. Yet, tea tree essential oil can be used for eye infections if done very carefully and in a very diluted form. This can be done as follows: put one drop of tea tree essential oil in a cup of warm water. Blend it well and then soak a cotton ball in this mixture. The cotton ball is then applied over the closed eye. A more complicated approach is to dissolve the tea tree essential oil in salt. You may recall that tears have a saline concentration twice that of blood (14g per kg). You can put a drop of tea tree essential oil into a teaspoon of salt, blend very well and then dilute this aromatic salt in 250 ml of warm distilled water. This aromatic saline water can be used locally for eye infections. Remember that if you see puss coming from the inside corners of the eyes, its origin is generally from the sinuses or the nose. Therefore it is advisable to disinfect the nostrils as well as the eyes, and this can be done using the same aromatic saline solution sprayed into both sides of the nose.

Temporary Dental Relief

Tooth infections are very painful and can be a serious threat to general health. In case of a tooth infection, the first thing you do is call your dentist. But it is rare to get an immediate appointment. Tea tree essential oil can help you get by until the dentist can see you. You can simultaneously control the infection and reduce the pain by putting a few drops of tea tree essential oil on a small cotton ball and placing it in direct contact with the tooth, between the cheek and the tooth. Many popular aromatherapy books recommend clove for this application, but I don't think they've ever really tried it. Clove essential oil can burn the gum tissue and also the throat if swallowed. My choice is to combine utility with safety, and tea tree remains the best option. If the pain is acute, a small amount of peppermint can be added to the cotton ball as well. I've done this several times on myself and with many patients with great success.

Recently a patient called me about her husband, a fireman, who had been suffering with a severe tooth infection for five days. The dentist had prescribed antibiotics, but for five days the situation had become progressively worse. She was familiar with essential oils and knew where to obtain therapeutic quality, so I explained how to make capsules for internal use, using tea tree essential oil as the main ingredient. I also instructed her how to put a blend of tea tree and peppermint on a cotton ball and place that between the cheek and the tooth. After just one day of this dual treatment, he reported significant improvement and reduction in pain.

This is really a significant process. It is most unfortunate that dentists and dental surgeons are not more familiar with the benefits of using essential oils in their work. If they would use essential oils as I have described on the gums and teeth after they perform oral surgery or an extraction, it would significantly reduce inflammatory reactions and the pain that accompanies them. Healing would no doubt proceed at a faster pace, and patients would experience much less discomfort. I look forward to the day when aromatic treatments will be commonly used in dentistry and oral surgery. It may happen sooner than you think, because there is a tradition of using clove essential oil in dentistry already.

In summary, I hope you can see that whenever you encounter a problem that would seem to require antibiotics, there is another effective option in tea tree essential oil. I encourage you to experiment with it. You will find that 1) if you use a very high quality essential oil like the ones available in my kits and 2) if you begin your applications immediately, you will be able to arrest the problem and begin to see almost immediate improvement. This improvement will continue until the problem is eliminated.

Chapter 8: Tropical Basil *(Ocimum basilicum)*

We now turn to the first of three oils in our second group. The essential oils in this second group—tropical basil, geranium, and lavender—have in common an antispasmodic effect. Physically, they can soothe and relieve tension, stress, and blockage in key body systems. There is also scientific evidence to support the idea that they have a similar effect on the psyche. The molecules that give these three essential oils their antispasmodic characteristics are from the families of ethers and esters.

Ethers and esters are completely absent from tea tree and eucalyptus radiata. There is a small amount of an ester called menthyl acetate in peppermint. The presence of this molecule in peppermint is part of the reason why peppermint has a soothing (antispasmodic) effect on the digestive system.

There are three general problem areas that I think of when health is impaired. They are toxemia, poor vitality, and blockages/tension. Invariably some or all of these conditions are involved in precipitating disease and malfunction. They often combine with each other to undermine general health. To resolve each of them requires a different type of action on the body. I will review each one separately.

Toxemia

The human body is literally filled with tubes. When you think about it, almost every system of the body uses a network of natural pipes to perform its function. The digestive system, the circulatory system, the respiratory and sinus system, the lymphatic system, the urinary system, the nervous system—all are built of tubes of various sizes and types. The skeletal system does not appear as a continuous tube, yet all bones are filled with marrow, making each bone a tube of sorts. My American colleague, Don Tolman, speaks often of the concept that most disease arises when these tubes become congested or clogged in some way. It is a condition he calls "congestive toxicosis." Medical doctors involved in natural medicine call it toxemia. The body's tubes can become obstructed fairly easily if we do not take proper care of them.

We all know what constipation is. Mucous often clogs the nasal and respiratory passages, resulting in colds and coughs. The number one cause of death in America is heart disease, which results when the walls of the arteries supplying the heart become so thickly coated with cholesterol that the heart's blood supply is reduced or stopped. One primary reason why our tubes become clogged is because the body is trying to eliminate poisons, toxins, and other unnatural material through those tubes.

When one system's tubes become clogged, sometimes other body systems try to compensate. Often they, in turn, get congested. It can become a vicious cycle. That is why we talk so much of whole body cleansing and detoxification. It goes well beyond intestinal activity. For chronic problems, we always include cleansing as part of the protocol, because it opens up the body's mechanisms for getting rid of problems. Exercise plays an important role in this process also.

Poor Vitality

This problem is often a genetic one. Our body's innate ability to absorb nutrients and use them efficiently to produce energy is affected by many hereditary factors. Still, there is much that can be done in by way of lifestyle habits to compensate for genetic weaknesses. I strongly maintain that a person born with limited vitality who gives proper care to his/her body through a responsible lifestyle will do better and feel better than one who has a tremendous genetic endowment yet makes poor lifestyle choices.

Blockage and tension

The problem referred to here is not the same as toxemia, explained above. This area has more to do with the energy flow in the body—a primary subject of Chinese medicine that most Western doctors still have not learned. In the same way that undue stress can create sore neck muscles, for example, blockages in energy flow through the body can limit the function of various organs, leading to tension, congestion and ultimately disease. Relieving this type of problem is critical in our world today, where we are faced with constant stress—not just from mental/emotional pressures, but also from physical stresses stemming from continuous noise, light, and air pollution.

These three factors—toxemia, poor vitality, and blockage/tension—often reinforce each other in a synergy of negativity that makes people sick. Essential oils can deal with all three problems both separately and simultaneously. The particular compounds or molecules that an essential oil contains determine what its primary benefits will be. Some work best in relieving congested tubes (such as the three oils in our first group), while others strengthen vitality. Still others are best suited for soothing muscles and organs, relieving tension and energy blockages (including the three oils in our second group). In fact, essential oils can be so specific in their action that they are best suited to a particular organ or body system. I have selected tropical basil, geranium, and lavender because they help relieve tension and blockages (antispasmodic) in the digestive system, circulatory system, and nervous systems, respectively.

We could say that the essential oils in the first group are more yang and those of the second group are more yin. The oils of the first group should be avoided in the evening because they tend to be energizing, while those of the second group are ideal for evening application because their effect is calming.

Having said this, I must repeat that nature is complex, and sometimes the rules are not that simple. Essential oils—often with hundreds of organic compounds—are far more complex in their effect than are allopathic drugs made of a single (usually synthetic) compound. When allopathic doctors read in an aromatherapy book that opposing properties can come from the same essential oil, they often label it rubbish and forget about it. Most medical and pharmaceutical professionals are not used to dealing with substances that are produced by life itself. Life is not as black-and-white as synthetic prescriptions are supposed to be. Many factors determine the activity of an essential oil in the body—the quantity used, whether they are diluted, if they are diluted in oil or water, the degree of dilution, how and where they are applied, the general health and receptivity of the patient, etc. This may seem overwhelming, but remember: nature is complex, so we don't have to be. By knowing and using some of the simple guidelines I will give you in this book, you can take advantage—safely—of the best blessings that essential oils have to offer.

The first question I get when I announce that tropical basil has an antispasmodic effect on the digestive system is "What about peppermint? I thought you just said peppermint was for helping the digestive system?" This question gives me an opportunity to contrast some important application differences between these two oils. It is very true that peppermint helps the stomach. As we mentioned earlier, peppermint contains a small amount of menthyl acetate, an ester that is antispasmodic. This compound is part of the reason why peppermint has some antispasmodic properties for the stomach.

However, there is a difference between solving an acute problem and supporting and enhancing regular function. Using an automobile analogy, we all try to learn how to do preventative maintenance on our cars so they will last longer and not break down unexpectedly. Nonetheless, sometimes cars do break down, and then we have no choice but to have the car towed to the mechanic and get it fixed. Internal intake of peppermint would be like this repair function. Internal use of tropical basil would fall into the preventative-maintenance category.

The active molecule in tropical basil that helps the digestive system belongs to a family known as phenol methyl ethers. Generally we just use the term ethers. This group of compounds differs from the esters group in that there are only two ether compounds commonly found in essential oils. By contrast, dozens of different types of esters are found in essential oils. Of the two ethers, one is transanethole and it is found in anise, star anise, and fennel seeds and the essential oils distilled from them.

The second ether is known as chavicol methyl ether. It is sometimes called estragole, after the French word for tarragon, which is *estragon.* Tarragon essential oil is very difficult to obtain, so it is sensible to turn to another aromatic plant with a high methyl chavicol content, and that plant is tropical basil. There are several other kinds of basil that are distilled for their essential oils, but their methyl chavicol content is lower. We select tropical basil to get maximum antispasmodic benefits for the digestive system.

Tropical basil seems to naturally focus its antispasmodic effect on the digestive system. This is what we call a tropism. If you open a bottle of high quality tropical basil and smell its aroma, you can sense immediately that its effect connects you with foods and the pleasure of eating. In my opinion, the easiest, most logical, and generally most pleasant way to use tropical basil to help the digestive system is not through breathing the aroma (though this is pleasant) or through topical applications (though this can also be very nice) but rather through ingesting.

In our aromatic training sessions in France, Rose Marie does a wonderful thing so the class can experience first-hand the effect of tropical basil. In a blender she combines, for each student, one teaspoon of honey, one drop of tropical basil essential oil and one cup of warm water. After mixing thoroughly, she serves each class member a cup of this tropical basil tea. We receive nothing but compliments about the extraordinary taste of this sweet beverage. In more intensive two-day sessions, when we share our lunch, we add a few drops of tropical basil essential oil to the salad dressing or invite students to place a tiny trace on fresh tomatoes. The response is always enthusiastic.

The taste of tropical basil can work well on both sweet and salty foods. One drop of tropical basil in a glass of tomato juice will surprise you! We do not use canned juice in our home, but when we travel by plane, we always complement our vegetarian dinners with a glass of tomato juice laced with a drop of tropical basil. It is very invigorating and pleasant to the taste buds as well as the stomach. Sometimes the stomach needs a little extra help when digesting airline food!

When you find yourself in a situation of worry or urgency or under some other type of tension while you are eating, even a nutritious meal can remain blocked in your digestive system, yielding little or no benefit to you. When you eat junk food you are a prime target for clogged tubes of one kind or another. Tropical basil can help this problem. By merely taking a few seconds to experience its aroma before eating, you will find an inclination to take on a more respectful, grounded attitude toward your meal. It is important when you eat to feel relaxed and joyful, thankful to nature for all that she offers us, thankful for those who prepared the food, thankful that you have food to eat at all.

This ideal of sharing a nutritious meal, in a spirit of joy and gratitude, with good friends or family is very difficult to achieve today. It is one of the important realities of health that has been sacrificed to the god of busy schedules. Use tropical basil to give you the extra help you need to enjoy your meals more. Its aroma alone can predispose your whole digestive system for better results as it harmonizes your mental state. Digestion for us human beings begins in our minds and in our sense organs. A great part of the pleasure in any sensual activity lies in the mental preparation and imagination that precedes the actual activity. Our capacity to delay the moment of gratification while we anticipate it can immensely enhance the pleasure we experience in the final act.

You can see this for yourself. Simply apply a trace of tropical basil on the back of your hand and breathe its aroma a few times, two minutes before eating a meal. This moment of pure pleasure will help both your stomach and your mind get prepared to receive the food. As outside tensions decline, you will be in a better condition to fully enjoy your meal.

When we rush like madmen to get through a quick (and usually non-nutritious) meal, our normal sensory experience that should be part of healthy eating and digestion is neglected. Many try to compensate for this by eating more food than they need—usually of the wrong kind—to satisfy their appetite. . This can lead to bingeing and become a broad and complex psychological problem over time. You will be surprised by the balance and regulation you will feel from the simple act of making tropical basil essential oil a part of your eating pattern. Essential oils—especially tropical basil—can help us recalibrate the normal systems of our body and eat in a more natural, healthful way. They can reeducate our senses. Again, life helping life.

The United States has the largest percentage of overweight people in the world. Yet though Americans are overfed in total calories, they are *underfed nutritionally.* The body tries to compensate for the absence of natural nutrition by prompting us to overeat refined, processed, or fast foods! The pattern is similar in many other industrialized countries. The normal sensual pleasure of eating natural food is lost.

Many are trying to solve their obesity by using restrictive diets, which remove even more of the sensory pleasure of eating! There is no hope of succeeding in reeducating our senses when the campaign is founded on additional denial/suppression of fundamental sensory needs. This is why dieters often end up bingeing. The way to change dietary habits is to create a program that will help us recapture and relish the sensory pleasure derived from eating healthy foods. In reality the driving force behind such a program is an honest determination to find ways to live life to its fullest.

There is a methodology for using essential oils to help people lose extra weight. It is much more involved than just smelling an aroma to suppress appetite. I believe the key to such a program is using the essential oils to help solidify new and better lifestyle patterns.

To understand how this can happen, let's consider how your brain works. Do this simple exercise with me:

1. First, close your eyes and remember a particularly beautiful scene. It might be a sunset, a view from lofty mountains, or a picture taken in a national park. Just close your eyes and remember a scene that was particularly pleasurable to you. Imagine every possible detail.
2. Second, close your eyes again and think of your favorite music, whether it's a symphony, a popular song, or a hymn. Imagine the exact arrangement of the music that you enjoy. Hear in your mind all the musical nuances.
3. Third, close your eyes again and think about lemon juice and how it tastes. Feel the acidity and the puckering that it creates in your mouth. This will usually cause a physical reaction in your mouth.
4. Lastly, close your eyes again and evoke the scent of your favorite essential oil. Remember it as keenly as you possibly can.

Most people find, curiously enough, that their imagination works vividly to bring up visual memories, auditory memories, and even taste memories. But imagining aromas is something our brains do not do well. You might be able to intellectually recall how you felt when breathing the essential oil aroma, but you cannot really relive the perception in the same way you can visualize the scene, hear the music or taste the lemon juice.

Do you understand the importance of this difference between the olfactory sense and the other senses? This makes our sense of smell unique from all the other senses. We need to have the actual aroma in our nostrils to fully re-experience the aroma. **This phenomenon demonstrates that our olfactory sense is a connection to honest reality.** It brings us into contact with the present moment; in the reality that surrounds us instead of the reality that is in our mental imaginations.

Seen in this way, essential oils are tools to reeducate our thinking away from the extreme quantitative/analytical approach to everything, to a more spontaneous/emotional approach, which forms the foundation of our behaviors. It is no surprise that certain aromas can arouse rich memories and intense feelings within us. Remember that the olfactory organs are closer to the brain than any others.

I believe that essential oils are one of the most priceless gifts we have from the plant kingdom. If you are very observant, you will notice that each time your nose catches the delicate scent of a quality essential oil, you may feel like sighing, or you may even feel the need to yawn. This is also a sign of your mind's reaction to the aroma. Your mind is letting go and opening up to the influence of the emotional message of the aromatic plant. You are neither in an offensive or defensive mode, but rather accepting and open to whatever thoughts are anchored with the aroma. Imagine the possibilities for overcoming self-defeating behaviors using the power of essential oils.

Before I get too carried away, let's return to a case history involving tropical basil. This incident was related in the book I wrote with Pierre Franchomme, *L'aromathérapie exactement*. While still in her early 40s, the wife of one of my medical colleagues developed severe rheumatoid arthritis. To keep her pain and discomfort under control, she consumed large doses of corticoid drugs. As you may know, rheumatoid arthritis is a very serious autoimmune condition wherein the body manufactures antibodies that destroy its own joints. This lady became interested in natural therapies and approached a wholistic natural physician about using some form of aromatic treatment. His prescription was to start a first-step treatment using a tropical basil emulsion in a Jacuzzi-type bath three times a week. After a few sessions, she experienced a remarkable decrease in both the pain and the stiffness of her joints, so much so that she was able to significantly reduce her large doses of allopathic drugs.

I relate this actual history not because I want you to think that tropical basil is a miraculous cure for this dreadful disease. It is not appropriate to expect sudden miracles from essential oils (though you should know that sometimes they do occur). In this case, the simultaneous relaxing action and the reality-connecting ability of the tropical basil played a significant role in triggering noticeable improvements. Your role, of course, is not to expect to treat serious diseases, but rather to help yourself and your family maintain a healthy lifestyle that incorporates regular and safe use of essential oils.

Lifestyle changes—Controlling eating patterns

Tropical basil can play a very helpful role in two other lifestyle areas that need further comment. One is in getting control over eating patterns. I touched on this earlier in this chapter. Let me reiterate that no long-term weight management program can be based on rejecting life and its legitimate pleasures. The only successful approach is to become more fully connected with those pleasures and to experience them with a peaceful and grateful heart. We should never feel guilty about expanding our ability to find joy in life. I believe our Creator absolutely intended for us to do this, and He gave us several basic guidelines on how to do it best.

I believe using tropical basil essential oil in the following simple program can have a profound effect on your success in changing eating habits. It has 3 simple points:

1. Any attempt at lifestyle change involves breaking an old habit and instituting a new behavior long enough that it becomes automatic. This usually takes three to four weeks, depending on which behaviorist you read. During this period there may be a struggle to maintain the habit, but usually within a month the new habit will be established.

2. Getting control over poor eating habits requires some knowl edge of nutrition and also requires that you work with quality, nutritious food. The processed food and junk food so prevalent in modern diets makes it impossible to experience the joy of good nutrition and keeps us imprisoned in a negative cycle of over-consumption, under-nutrition, and poor health. You will

need to learn enough to select a correct menu of natural foods that you can snack on and prepare for whatever meals you have. This may involve eliminating many foods that have hitherto been important to you. Your new meals can be quite small, especially if your are eating or snacking more than 3 times per day. All programs require variety, so you will need to adjust your menu each day.

3. Lastly—and this is the unique twist that tropical basil pro vides—each time you eat, take 30 seconds to go through the following ritual. Just before you commence eating, take your bottle of tropical basil essential oil, and open it. Use a dropper to place a trace on the back of your hand, then move your hand back and forth slowly 12" to 18" from your nose, allowing the aroma to float to your nostrils. Breathe it in deeply. Give in to it. Then let your mind be filled with ideas similar to the following. You may want to rewrite this script in your own words, or just try to recreate these thoughts in a new way each time. Some of you may want to combine it with whatever prayer or "grace" you offer as you begin your meal.

> *I open myself to the joy of eating the right foods in the right proportions. I allow myself to get every bit of pleasure possible from the food I eat. I thank the Creator for all that makes this meal possible and for this essential oil that reconnects me to life and to others. Out of respect for my body's health, I commit to adjust my eating patterns to match a healthy pattern. Let this food be blessed and let it be transformed into positive energy in my body and my mind, leading to positive thoughts, loving feel ings, kind words, and helpful actions.*

This last step will make a tremendous difference in your ability to follow through with your lifestyle change, because you will be incorporating the power of aromatic stimulation and olfactory perception into the program. Plus you will have the benefit of the aromatic molecules in tropical basil that will strengthen your digestive mechanism and prepare it to desire good nutrition.

Should you still feel some tension or discomfort in following this program, whether psychological or physical, there is more that can be done, as follows:

A. Neck massage: Pour six drops of carrier oil into the empty cap of the tropical basil bottle. Add one drop of tropical basil essential oil. Blend it by placing the lid between your thumb and forefinger and turning it back and forth three or four times. Sit in front of a table or desk, so you can bend your head forward with your elbows resting on the table. Apply a few drops to the nape of the neck and begin massaging very close to the spine itself, using a downward motion. Rub downward in 2-3" strokes moving laterally slightly with each downward stroke, first on the left side, then on the right. You will discover that just one minute of this neck massage brings deep relief, not only in the muscles of the neck, but to all the tensions of the body and the mind. Of course, it's wonderful if you are in a situation that you can have a friend or partner do this massage for you, but if not, it is easy to do by yourself.

B. Auricular massage points: With a trace of the essential oil, massage the reflex area on the ear corresponding to the cervical spine. This point is located on the lower back cartilage area of the ear just after the tragus on the helix. It should be massaged in an ascending movement, primarily on the back of the ear. (See diagram). Another important location is the cartilage groove just below the ear opening. It is the area connected to the hypophysis and the hypothalamus. With a trace of tropical basil essential oil massage the area between the tragus and the antitragus, on the inside.

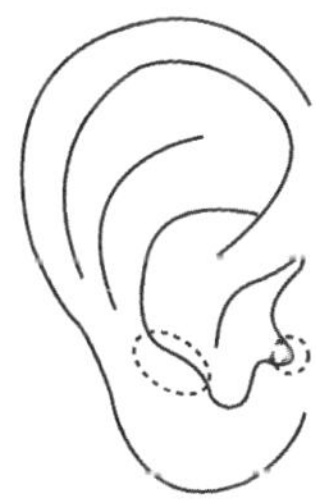

C. Brush your teeth. After a meal, small food particles usually remain lodged in the teeth. If you do not clean your teeth, the saliva in your mouth continues to contain minute food particles that can continue to trigger digestive processes, stimulating your appetite unconsciously. Once your mouth is completely free of any food particles and fresh from using a safe, natural aromatic toothpaste, it will be easier to refrain from temptations to eat unhealthy foods. Many of my female patients who had real problems with bingeing found that this simple step made a big difference in the success of their re-education program.

The above steps will go a long way toward breaking down any nervous tension that may arise as you change your old habits. None of these recommendations requires any serious amounts of time and generally they can be performed almost anywhere, even at work during a break. They help you build self-mastery. This is not a passive program! It is a program that mobilizes your self-determination by enhancing mental power, tension release, and digestive support. You are not punishing yourself or your body; nor are you denying yourself any right to enjoy and appreciate food. On the contrary, you are on a course that will slowly but surely increase your pleasure in eating and acting in a spirit of love and respect for your body.

The real goal in this program is only indirectly to lose weight. The fundamental objective is to become fully alive. You will start to love life again, and life will in turn be kind to you. Never think that these feelings are selfish! As you become more in tune with the process, you will find yourself thinking and feeling greater concern for those around you. Again, life helping life. Helping yourself is only a first step toward your mission to help others.

Lifestyle Effects–Constipation, Colitis, Irritable Bowel

Tropical basil essential oil is a wonderful aid in soothing and strengthening the digestive system and can be used to improve the whole lower abdominal area through massage. In Ayurvedic medicine this area is influenced through the second Chakra or energy center. An effective massage on the second Chakra is performed on both the front and back of the body. As you know, when I talk of using essential oils in a massage, I mean they will be diluted in carrier oil. In this case, count three to five drops of tropical basil essential oil in a tablespoon of carrier oil. Begin the second Chakra massage on the back, at the level of the fourth lumbar vertebra. Massage along each side of the spine in a downward motion. This will take only a minute or two, but it is important to begin on the backside. If you are alone, you can do it on yourself by using both thumbs on either side of the spine.

The second stage of this massage is done directly on the front part of the lower abdomen. Take a few drops of the diluted essential oil on the fingertips and apply gently, starting at a point about 2" directly below the navel. The movement should be in expanding clockwise circles, making about 12 revolutions to reach the outer area of the abdomen. Repeat this cycle of 12 circles starting at the original point each time, increasing the pressure very slightly on each cycle. This massage is easy to perform on yourself and is recommended to help you get acquainted with your abdominal organs. For women this massage will have the added benefit of soothing the uterus, fallopian tubes, and ovaries.

You will probably find that certain areas are quite tender. Do not be overly concerned about this. Simply continue this gentle massage at regularly scheduled intervals. You will discover that, after a few sessions, the tenderness will decrease, even though the massage pressure may increase. This is a sure sign that the unblocking is under way deep inside.

This same massage technique can be applied slightly higher on the abdomen, starting at the solar plexus just under the sternum. Remember to start on the equivalent area on the back and spine first, then do the massage on the front. This technique when performed regularly can bring great relief to intestinal problems, especially if integrated with a full program of nutritional improvement.

Dysmenorrhea

A very common problem in the lower abdomen that affects many females is the problem of dysmenorrhea or painful cramping during menstrual periods. Here again, tropical basil is well suited to help the problem. Because the pain involved with this problem is intense, I do not dilute the tropical basil essential oil for this application, in order to get rapid penetration and faster relief.

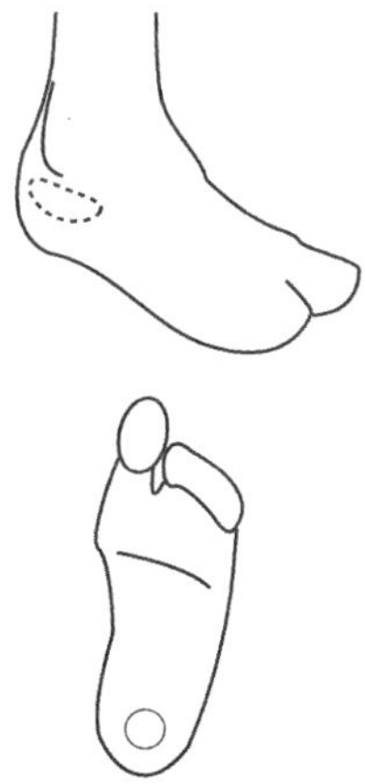

We are of course taking advantage of the antispasmodic characteristic of tropical basil. Menstrual cramps are usually spasms that occur in the uterus. A few drops of undiluted tropical basil essential oil applied gently to the lower abdomen are usually sufficient to get the pain under control. Additional applications and light massage with diluted essential oil can be administered if desired. Another helpful step is to massage the diluted essential oil on the reflex point for the uterus on the feet, which is located on the lower sides of the heels and directly under the heel itself, where you find the master point for the entire genital system. It is often helpful to massage the hypophysis point, too, at the center of the inferior side of the big toe.

Recently our daughter Magali experienced this very problem and she came to me asking for help in getting relief. As she sat in a recliner, I applied 10 drops of neat tropical basil essential oil on her lower abdomen with no real massage, simply a gentle touch in clockwise circles. I used the essential oil neat to get the fastest possible absorption for quick relief. After applying 10 drops neat, I mixed three drops tropical basil essential oil in 10 drops of carrier oil and used this to massage the reflex points on the feet as described above. I massaged her feet for about 10 minutes, at which point she began to feel the number and intensity of spasmodic waves decrease. Within 15 minutes after starting the treatment, the pain was under control. Within 30 minutes, Magali was pain free.

Some additional essential oils work well for this problem also, including the other two oils in our second group—lavender and geranium. Another essential oil that is known for its female support is clary sage. Any female who is prone to this monthly suffering can help herself by applying one or more of these essential oils to the lower abdomen, twice a day, three to four days before the start of menstruation. Three to five drops should be used for each application. In many cases, after a few of these treatments, the body changes its way of reacting, and the intensity and length of the pain tapers off gradually, sometimes completely disappearing.

Hay Fever

The medical name for hay fever is spasmodic rhinitis. This illness tends to be allergy-related, so extra caution and testing should be done for sensitivity to essential oils. But the antispasmodic tropical basil oil can be used to provide some relief. I recommend a blend, which you can make from your single oils, as follows:

10 drops tropical basil
3 drops eucalyptus radiata
3 drops balsam fir
2 drops peppermint

If desired you can add two drops of lavender or lemon to this blend. The easiest way to use this is to place a drop directly on the tongue, let it mix with saliva for a minute or two and then swallow. This can be repeated as often as is necessary to control the problem. Short-term results are usually very good, but long-term relief for this problem requires a complete treatment protocol.

Hiccups

Hiccups, too, are a form of spasm. For serious cases, a drop or two of undiluted tropical basil oil applied to the nape of the neck and a trace applied directly to the tongue will usually bring relief. One of my patients called one evening asking my advice for his son, who had been taken to the hospital with a trauma. The trauma injury was completely under control, but the event had triggered a permanent hiccup response that had become painful because it would not stop. No one at the hospital knew what to do. I advised him to apply tropical basil essential oil to the back of his neck and a trace on his tongue. To the total surprise of everyone on the hospital staff, this simple measure stopped the hiccups within a few minutes!

Chapter 9: Geranium *(Pelargonium x asperum)*

Geranium has a confusing name. There are many types of geranium plants, but in France we actually refer to this essential oil as geranium. This name is clearly closer to its Latin name. But traditionally this essential oil was called geranium, and it continues today. This plant is related to, but is not like the flowering potted geraniums you grow in your house or yard.

Geranium essential oil has long been used in the perfume industry. As mentioned before, this essential oil is antispasmodic, and, like tropical basil, it has a tropism.

Introduce geranium to your olfactory sensors by opening the vial and holding it about 10" from the nose. This powerful essential oil has a strong scent, so do not bring it too close to the nose. As the aroma meets your nose, let go and breathe deeply. Accept it completely and let it penetrate your being. Try to sense where it goes.

A Heart-centered Essential Oil

For most people, this aroma seems to proceed to the very lowest part of the throat and then centers itself in the center of the upper thorax—the area of the heart. And indeed, geranium, or scented pelargonium, has a strong tropism for the throat chakra and the heart chakra. Keep in mind that when we use the term 'heart' in this context, we are including not only its physiological meaning (our body's biological pump) but also its emotional and psychological meanings. In the Ayurvedic chakra system, the heart chakra is the symmetrical center of all the chakras. The throat-heart area that feels activated when you breathe geranium and the impulse to yawn (what I call the 'yawn reflex') that sometimes accompanies the aroma indicates the rapid influence this essential oil can have in the body.

If you have had exposure to other geranium essential oils, you may immediately recognize that the aroma from the essential oil in my kit triggers a different feeling, a deeper response, than the geranium oils you have experienced. This is because most commercially available geranium essential oil is—for economic reasons—grown and distilled in

China, the largest producer and exporter of essential oils in the world. When we analyze the chemical composition of Chinese geranium oil we find the dominant compound is citronnelol. Another important ingredient in geranium essential oils, geraniol, is lower than citronnelol.

By contrast, the geranium essential oil found in my kit is produced in Egypt. The dominant compound in this essential oil is geraniol, with citronnelol being secondary. This reverse proportion between the two main alcohols accounts for most of the difference in aroma and the difference in effect on the body. I do not mean to imply that there is anything wrong with Chinese pelargonium. I am only explaining that because of this chemical composition difference, the Egyptian geranium has a much deeper effect from an energy point of view.

I have not always been a big fan of geranium. In fact, I have only been using it in my medical aromatic practice for the last few years. In the French orientation of using essential oils for medical purposes, there is limited use for perfume essential oils. However, through my study of English-style aromatherapy, I discovered the real biological power of this wonderful essential oil. I chose to include it in my singles essential oils kit primarily for medical reasons.

Cicatrization—Closing Physical and Emotional Wounds

There is a need in an aromatherapy kit to have an essential oil to apply on bleeding cuts or lesions in the skin that will help close the wound as it disinfects. The oil I traditionally use for this purpose is labdanum. However, labdanum essential oil is rare and very expensive, so it was not appropriate for a high volume kit like the one I have developed.

Geranium—which is far more economical—has many of the characteristics of labdanum, plus it has an extra benefit: its action actually helps to cleanse an open wound. How does it do this? You will note that when you put a few drops on a cotton ball and apply it to a wound, the bleeding seems to increase at first, for a short time. This action helps to cleanse the wound, eliminating foreign matter and microbes that may have penetrated the skin. After this first phase, however, the action changes and the second effect of the essential oil is to stop the bleeding. This two-stage action is ideally suited for treating bleeding wounds.

After applying the essential oil with a cotton ball, the wound can be wrapped with a cling film and then covered with a bandage. This dressing can be renewed after 12 hours, depending on need.

In addition to its effect on bleeding, the geranium essential oil will disinfect and accelerate the wound healing process. This is ideally suited to first aid applications and is the primary reason why it should be in the singles kit and certainly in your microkit pouch.

We can learn much about the emotional or subtle side of this essential oil by using an analogy on the physical wound. When we think of the emotional arena, there is a part of our being that feels cut when we are psychologically wounded. Often we need a way to heal emotional wounds that hurt our heart. I am indebted to my good friend, Martin Henglein from Germany, for explaining the way that geranium essential oil can heal the emotional heart. I invited him to speak at the First International Symposium on Integrated Aromatic Medicine in Grasse, France, in March 1998. In his presentation he explained that whenever a severe psychological shock occurs, inhaling the aroma of geranium essential oil provides great help in limiting the mental and physical consequences of the shock. I would suggest, in addition to breathing the essential oil aroma, applying one drop of essential oil on the breastbone, from the top to the xyphoid process, and another drop over the heart area, using gentle clockwise motions.

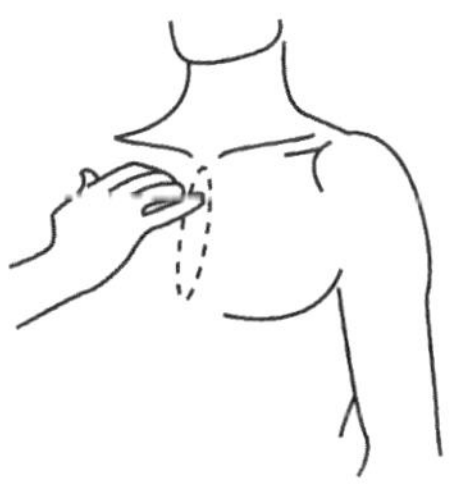

Remember that you do not rub a drop of neat essential oil into the skin! You gently and lightly tap it on allowing it to penetrate almost by itself. It will be absorbed through the skin without any pressure or friction. Your technique should be a magic touch accompanying a magic essential oil in cases of mental trauma

With this background you should be able to visualize the physical and emotional healing action of geranium, bringing together both sides of a physical cut in the skin, and doing the same with body and soul in the case of a psychological wound, relinking and healing. As earlier mentioned, the sooner the essential oil treatment can be started after physical or mental trauma, the better effect can be obtained. However, geranium can still have a definite beneficial effect even a few hours or a few days after an emotional trauma. Since the urgency of the moment will have passed at this stage, you can take more time to converse with the person about the nature of the shock he/she has been through and offer feelings of empathy and concern. Representing and providing the blessings of essential oils to your friends and family means that you should carry the same selfless spirit that the essential oils do. We are here on this earth, first of all, to help and to serve in the best possible way, not to prove that we are more correct or wiser than others. If we keep this priority foremost, we can confidently give liberally of ourselves, knowing that whatever we give away will, in time return many-fold greater.

It is important, in the context of applying essential oils generally, but especially with geranium, to understand deeper the vital process of breathing. Remember that the thoracic area, centered by the heart chakra, is the location of both the heart and the lungs. These two critical organs function together in permanent synchronicity, performing their cycles in a ratio of about one to three or four (breaths to heart beats) as long as life continues!

The spiritual meaning of the act of breathing is: freely allow yourself to receive and freely allow yourself to give. If I try to keep my air inside all the time, in a selfish way, I will die. I cannot receive fresh new air because I cannot expel the old air. This pattern has lessons for us in interpersonal relationships. Learning to give is a wonderful and challenging skill to master; yet learning to receive can also be a challenge. Both are required for breathing; both are required for a full life. It is common to meet people who only think of giving to others, yet seem incapable of accepting anything. It is wonderful to give, but refusing to receive is not a fair attitude. It is a misinterpretation of charity. If you want to be able to give more over a longer time, you must learn to receive, too.

By now you are realizing that I am completely fascinated with the great lessons that aromatic plants and essential oils teach us about life and about reharmonizing ourselves. Geranium teaches us about heart. It focuses its action on the upper thorax/heart chakra, where we see the heart and lungs performing constantly in harmony. When we connect the spirit of our heart with the spirit of breathing, we discover the great lesson that we must receive in the same proportion as we learn to give.

Skin Care

Besides its profound effect on the physical and mental heart, geranium essential oil is a wonderful aid to skin care. Remember that it greatly accelerates cicatrization of a cut. Its ability to heal the skin makes it a prime essential oil for daily skin care. You can easily create your own gentle aromatic oil to keep your skin looking its very best, as follows:

> Fill a 20-ml vial with 15 ml of a high quality, cold pressed vegetable oil. (For oily skin, hazelnut oil works well) Add to this 5-ml of jojoba oil (which is not a real oil, but a vegetable wax). Lastly, add 4-5 drops of geranium essential oil (about a 0.5% concentration) and mix well.

For a very small investment, this recipe you have just mixed is probably as effective as any skin lotion you can buy in the store. All you are missing is the expensive package it comes in and paying the extra cost to support expensive advertising!

Going one step further, you can enhance the beauty effect of your natural lotion by massaging it on specific reflex areas of the face. In so doing you receive both the local benefit and a reflex benefit. Your face is a powerful reflex area. It has many different reflex points in it, and I will show you how to work with four basic ones. These areas I will describe are from the book Healing with *Color Zone Therapy* by Joseph Corvo and Lilian Verner-Bonds, (Crossing Press, 1998).

1. The first reflex area is used to stimulate healthy bowel action. After applying a few drops of your geranium skin lotion on your middle fingers, massage in a circular movement along the ridge of the cheek bone, starting from the outside (about 1-inch down from the outside corners of the eyes) moving inward until you reach the edges of the nose. Repeat this four times, always working from the outside in, on both sides at the same time. If you massage from the inside to the outside, you will tend to block the secretions of the sinuses, instead of helping them drain.

2. The second reflex area is used to stimulate the spleen and the stomach. Find the ridge that runs from your nose to the middle of your upper lip, as shown. Massage this area with your special lotion for 20 seconds. You should be able to feel the gums underneath.

3. The third reflex area is used to stimulate the pancreas. A pancreas that functions properly plays a major role in helping the digestive system work properly, and that in turn will help increase the health and glow of the skin. These two areas are on the two sides of the lower lip, as shown. Massage from the corners of the lower lip to the center and back. This can be repeated several times. You should feel your lower gums doing this massage.

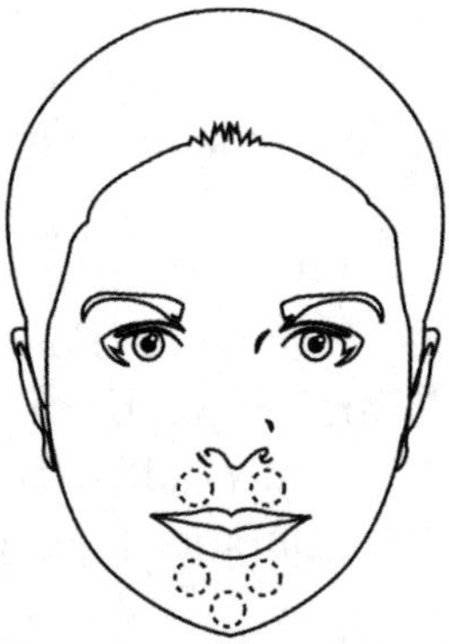

4. The fourth reflex area supports the first one in building healthy bowel function. Regular bowel movements play a crucial role in keeping the skin healthy. The accumulation of impurities inside the bowels is first and foremost perceived on the skin of the face! Put a drop of your lotion on the middle finger and massage the point at the indent in the chin, rotating clockwise with modest pressure for 30 seconds.

Massaging these four reflex points can easily be done in a couple of minutes. If done every day, these exercises will amplify, through reflex stimulation, the effect of simple topical application. Of course, you should also apply the lotion in small amounts to the other parts of the face. But remember to carefully avoid the eye areas and the eyelids. This very sensitive skin requires other kinds of preparations than an essential oil. Also, remember the safety concern about keeping essential oils—even diluted ones—well away from the eyes. Finally, remember the importance of massaging the nape of the neck in a downward movement. This will help unblock and unlock the portion of the spine that controls the front side of the heart area.

Normalizing Body Fluids

Another of geranium's special abilities in the human body is that of regulating or rather balancing the amount of fluid in body tissues. When out of balance, the body often stores more fluid than it should, causing joints, limbs, torsos and faces to swell and become puffy-looking. Too much fluid accumulates from overeating, inadequate exercise, severe inflammation and hormone imbalances. We will see that geranium can assist in all such situations, but of course, the ultimate solution is not a temporary relief, but a lifestyle that will not allow the problem to recur. This invariably involves some degree of nutritional correction.

A most memorable lesson in how geranium helps the body regulate its fluids occurred when I accidentally smashed my finger. The injury was very severe, imbedding several metallic particles inside the finger. But I determined to treat the problem entirely with essential oils and green clay. My methods controlled the infection quite well, but the problem was inflammation and swelling. I had to go show my hand to a specialist, and while I was quite confident of the job I had done with the infection, the inflammation problem was both painful but embarrassing. My forefinger swelled to almost twice its normal size from the inflammation and accumulation of lymphatic fluid. It was extremely tender and stiff. I could not bend it at all because of the pain. Frankly, it looked a bit like a stuffed sausage.

As I was sitting in my car in the parking lot minutes before the appointment, I took out my microkit and applied a few drops of geranium to the length of my afflicted forefinger. To my amazement, a transformation took place in my finger so rapidly that I could almost see it happen. As the essential oil penetrated, my finger began to slowly limber up. The swelling declined. In the space of about one minute, I went from zero movement to some modest pain-free movement in that finger. Within twenty minutes, I could bend my finger almost 40 degrees. It was such a relief. With this quick response, I was able to show my finger to the specialist with some pride that I had controlled both the infection and the swelling with essential oils and green clay. We decided there was no need to intervene with allopathic methods and the treatment was completed as it had started.

This experience was for me an incredible witness of the draining power of geranium essential oil. When you read in aromatherapy books that geranium essential oil has the power to help eliminate excess body fluids, this is not just somebody's opinion. This is a real power inherent in this wonderful essential oil.

PMS

Another rebalancing type problem is that of PMS, where hormones need to be balanced. Scented pelargonium is a staple essential oil used in treating this very complex problem. A whole book could be written on it. Let me just say that we know geranium essential oil can help with water retention, a common symptom with PMS. But secondly, the action of this essential oil goes much deeper than a simple diuretic. Geranium essential oil works in a subtle way on the overall balance of the pyscho-neuro-endocrine system. When turning to complex, living products like geranium essential oil, or any other essential oil, one is obliged to think in terms of highly complex interactions between systems which themselves are highly complex. The potential outcomes become numerous when you start to implement therapies like a full-body massage. Medical aromatherapy will never yield all its secrets to purely analytical thinking. I feel quite comfortable with this thought.

Last week I saw for the second time a female patient in her thirties who had come to me 60 days earlier for help in rebalancing her female hormones. Her problem was basically one of PMS, marked by fluid retention and great emotional tension prior to menstruation, among other things. I asked her to apply three drops of neat geranium essential oil to her lower abdomen every morning for the first 21 days of her cycle, then stop for the week that menstruation occurred. What surprised me most when I saw her this second time was that she really looked different. The best description I can give it is that she looked less swollen. She seemed much more toned, less dilated in a general sense. It was not that she had lost weight. Weight reduction was not the purpose of her aromatic care. The point is simply that geranium essential oil changes the way the body handles fluids. The medical word for this property is astringent, meaning that it tightens, it compresses, you could even say it wrings the water out of the tissues.

To conclude, let me give you a wonderful formula for an essential oil blend that you can make with three essential oils in your singles kit. This blend is very well suited to increase the draining power of geranium (geranium) essential oil. While geranium essential oil tastes quite peculiar in the mouth, blending it with these other essential oils makes it more palatable. Absorbing a drop of the blend can reinforce and synergize all the external applications you make to rebalance the body's fluids.

Here is the recipe:

20 drops of lemon essential oil
10 drops of balsam fir essential oil
10 drops of geranium essential oil

There are a number of ways this blend can be taken internally. I recommend taking one or two drops per day, blended in a soy yogurt or in stewed fruit. It will give a very nice fragrance as well as an interesting flavor to both the yogurt and the fruit. Remember to pause to smell the aroma before eating.

Chapter 10: Lavender *(Lavandula angustifolia)*

The lavender essential oil in my singles kit is some of the highest quality lavender available anywhere in the world. As you open the bottle and allow its aroma to float up to your nose, you will immediately sense its softness and gentleness, and its penetrating purity. This lavender essential oil is very different from the lavender commonly sold in stores. When you compare its aroma with those of commercial "lavenders" you will discern a real difference. Why is this so?

First of all, most of the essential oil of lavender sold in the US is actually not lavender at all, but a hybrid plant known as lavandin. If you buy a bottle of essential oil in the US and the label says lavender, but does not also give the Latin name of *Lavandula angustifolia,* then it probably is lavandin. I will explain more about this later. Secondly, a considerable amount of lavender essential oil is actually diluted instead of being full-strength, pure lavender essential oil. Thirdly, very little of the lavender essential oil available is certified organic, and therefore free of all poison residue from herbicides, fungicides, insecticides, and commercial fertilizers.

The lavender flowers for my essential oil are grown in the Drôme Valley, located in southeast France between the Alps and the Mediterranean Sea. Our home is located in this same area. Every summer we watch first-hand the harvesting and distilling of these marvelous flowers. It is so commonplace here that many take this phenomenon for granted and forget what a miracle it really is. Many lavender fields are within an hour's drive of our home. And there are dozens of distillers here.

The distiller of my lavender essential oil is a personal friend of mine. His may be the finest essential oil produced in the province. The flowers are grown in organic fields certified by the European Ecocert system. Distillation takes place in a newly built still that is completely computer controlled to make the process very gentle, extracting the largest number of constituents. It yields true medical aromatherapy grade essential oil. The quality is tangible. You can sense it in the penetrating aroma, and you can feel it whenever it touches your skin.

When you have an essential oil of this quality, you must remember that it can be and should be used very sparingly. A small trace will go a very long way from a therapy standpoint. Unfortunately, the converse is true also: if you have poor quality oil, you can bathe in it and it will not help.

This kind of quality also has a price. My oil kit may seem more expensive than other essential oil sets, but once you have experienced the exceptional quality, you will agree it is worth every penny.

Let's return to the subject of lavandin. For years lavandin has been sold as lavender, even though they are different species. When you compare the aromas of the two species you find that true lavender essential oil has a milder and much deeper aroma. If the aromas were sounds, I would say that true lavender has a lower pitch than lavandin. If the aromas were touches, I would say the lavandin has stronger pressure. Lavandin seems to evoke a yawing reflex quickly and easily. With lavender the feeling is that you must take a little more time, allowing the lavender aroma to reach deep levels in the lungs and the mind before the yawing reflex occurs.

True lavender only grows naturally at elevations of 700 meters above sea level and higher. Most of the hybrids grow well at lower elevations. Some wild lavender species grow naturally at low elevations, such as spike lavender *(Lavandula latifolia),* which grows on my farm at 300 meters above sea level. Here again, spike lavender essential oil is very different from true lavender essential oil.

In fact, lavandin is a cross (hybrid) between spike lavender and true lavender. This can happen naturally through the pollination efforts of bees, or it can happen commercially through the efforts of growers. Whenever you create a hybrid like this between two different species, you introduce an "x" between the genus and species names. The Latin name of lavandin is thus *Lavandula x intermedia.*

Why do growers and distillers work so much with lavandin? Because the lavandin species is a hybrid that can produce up to 10 times more essential oil from the same amount of plant material. This has tremendous ramifications if you are using the essential oil for scenting candles, soap, pot pourri, or perfume. Lavandin is not a bad essential oil; it is just different chemically from lavender. It is wonderfully suited for recreational fragrancing. On a limited, purely physical level, sometimes a high quality organic lavandin essential oil can work as well or even better than true lavender, because it has some camphor in it. This is especially true when massaging a diluted essential oil on the muscles and joints or when treating the respiratory system. But there are several other exceptional oils for these purposes.

In an effort to improve yields for recreational fragrancing and perfumery, growers here have created several more lavender hybrids in addition to lavandin. In actuality these hybrids have replaced many true lavender fields, and today true lavender is a small percentage of the total lavender crop in France. On the wholesale market, true lavender essential oil will typically cost at least 4 to 5 times more than lavandin essential oil.

So why did I then select true lavender for my kit? One reason is that true lavender is safer for use on infants and small children. But more importantly, *the message in true lavender essential oil is primarily an emotional one, not a physical one.* You cannot obtain the same emotional benefits from lavandin as you do from true lavender. For anyone interested in the vibrational medicinal benefits of aromatherapy, only true lavender will yield good results. If you have never used lavender principally for emotional reasons, you are awaiting a marvelous experience.

Applications for the Mind

Because lavender is such an exceptionally versatile oil, and so effective for a multitude of health uses, most authors are quick to exploit this oil as they would a "miracle pill" and ignore its exceptional non-physical applications. But I am going to break with the customary sequence of most aromatherapy books and discuss some of the non-physical applications of lavender first, and then follow with its medical applications.

Because of its unique chemistry, lavender has the wonderful ability to help create balance between the analytical and the intuitive or emotional sides of our personalities.

In high quality true lavender essential oil, the amount of linalyl acetate exceeds the amount of linalool. The balance of the two components has a major influence on the effect of the essential oil. We find that true lavender grown at higher altitudes has a higher linalyl acetate content than lavender grown at lower altitudes. Each makes an important contribution: the higher the linalool content, the greater the calming action of the essential oil; the higher the linalyl acetate content, the greater stimulation, balancing and harmonizing effect on the higher centers in the brain and the mind.

The role of esters is to unblock, unlock, and open. This opening effect on the mind helps in letting go of old stresses, problems and irritations, while becoming more receptive or more conscious of new and different realities. As in breathing, we exhale the used air and inhale the new fresh air. In this case it is happening in the brain.

Our intellect works through conscious, analytical, rational thought. But the spirit receives inspiration, often suddenly. These enlightenments are often described as solutions or ideas that just "pop into our heads." Some teachers suggest that our subconscious mind has a strong connection to the source of such inspiration. Some of us are naturally more gifted in receiving such information, but each of us can choose to discipline ourselves in ways that will enhance this universal capacity. Essential oils can assist in this, and clearly the essential oil of choice for this purpose is true lavender.

Aromatically-assisted Dreaming

Often the ideas that inspire us come during or just after sleeping. Sometimes they come in the form of conscious dreams; other times just as feelings. We often awake, knowing we had some kind of a significant and real experience, even if only in our minds. We know very little about exactly what process is taking place in our minds or why. But I do know that true lavender essential oil has (a) a calming and sedative effect on the mind, often helping induce sleep, and (b) the simultaneous ability to open our minds and souls to fresh ideas. So, I recommend to you a technique which I call "aromatically-assisted dreaming." The effects of this technique will surprise you.

Here is how to proceed:

1. It is important that you define clearly and repeatedly in your mind the problem that you want to solve, or the kind of help you need to meet a challenge you are facing. Before retiring for sleep, take your true lavender and inhale its aroma. Consider with gratitude the processes that created the plants. Consider the human connections that brought it to you.
2. Apply one drop to the center of your forehead, one inch above the eyebrow line. No massage is needed. Simply touch the drop to you forehead and allow it to penetrate.
3. Apply one drop to the throat area, over the Adam's apple and allow it to absorb spontaneously.
4. Apply one drop to the top of the head.
5. Apply a drop to a small cotton ball and place it between the first and second toes, the reflexology point for the brain.

You can use any one or all of the above. Don't expect something to happen every time. But if you are in a receptive state of mind, in some cases you will awake in the morning with a very clear memory of a dream that may shed light on how to approach your challenge. Or, it may help you confidently visualize yourself as you want to become—calm, sincere, loving, and beloved, capable of serving and inspiring others, etc.

At other times, you may not remember anything specific, but you will wake up with such a wonderful feeling that you know you are somehow different: you see life in a new way, you feel yourself more open, clearer, brighter, more confident in yourself, in others and in the ultimate goodness of life. Problems you may have thought impossible to solve are perceived in a new way that evokes reasonable solutions.

Aromatically-assisted Thinking, Pondering, and Meditating

A similar technique, which I call "aromatically-assisted thinking" can be used while awake as a form of regular emotional hygiene. All of us need to take more time to pause and think about things. It helps our inner growth. From a mental health standpoint, it is probably many times more important to take time, each day, to cleanse your soul and elevate your spirits, than it is to brush your teeth and comb your hair.

To do this, apply a trace of your true lavender essential oil just below the nostrils. Immediately the air you inhale will be filled with its sweet scent.

You are free to ponder the expanses of eternity or the realities of the moment. Think of the meaning you want to give your life. Think of your loved ones and your deep caring feelings that are sometimes difficult to express verbally. Resolve to ask forgiveness as you resolve to forgive. For those who are religious, it is natural to think of this as prayer.

I do not claim that lavender essential oil creates some sort of spiritual connection. What you ponder is completely the choice of your conscious mind. But this beautiful oil does enhance the mind's ability to stretch and open, facilitating the depth and effectiveness of your quiet, meditative moments.

Mind-enhancing Massage

A final way to use the mental/emotional power of lavender essential oil is through body massage, using a 2.5% solution in carrier oil (6-8 drops neat essential oil mixed in 1 tablespoon of carrier oil). Some basic training in simple massage technique is important, but there is far more to this than technique. This can be a profound experience if it is done in the proper spirit of respect and reverence for this wonderful oil.

When the massage is given or received by someone you love it can open your heart as few other things can. It is my fondest wish that everyone who is open to it, will be able to receive this supreme aromatic experience from loving hands and a loving and unselfish heart. The only thing that compares with receiving this special massage is giving it. Both participants discover new meaning to the word ecstasy.

A Message for All Religions

I am sometimes asked by well-meaning people, particularly devout Christians, if I am trying to create some kind of a new religion or sect when I speak of the psychological aspects of essential oils. I want all to understand clearly that my intent is always to teach the principles of aromatic health in a way that will be consistent with and harmonize with whatever religious position you may have, be it Protestant,

Catholic, Muslim, Buddhist, Shinto, Mormon, agnostic, or even atheist. It becomes difficult for me semantically to explain the concepts that nature and essential oils teach us without using many of the words that are common to religious dialogue.

My health message is not dramatically different than what is being taught by hundreds of other natural health professionals worldwide. It is unique, I think, in that it incorporates my special understandings acquired through 23 years of clinical experience with essential oils. One of the overriding realities that clinical practice has taught me is that those patients who have some kind of sincere spiritual orientation, with or without formal religious affiliation, have better health. They are (a) more inclined to respect their physical bodies and take care of them, and (b) are more successful in achieving health improvement as they implement various natural techniques, whether aromatic or otherwise.

My conclusion is this: it is in the best interest of my patients for me to encourage them in combining both physical and *spiritual* effort in the management of their health. My medical experience teaches me there is a spiritual/mental side to health, and that our souls need support as we seek to heal or preserve the health of our bodies.

What I am doing with aromatic medicine must not be considered in any way as the creation of a religion or sect. The last thing I want to create is a substitute for the deeply-felt religions I have come to respect. On the contrary, I encourage my patients to embrace spiritual concepts because this helps them heal and stay healthy. My experience gives me an opportunity to deliver a unique and relatively undiscovered message. I compare myself to a composer who is driven to compose his own unique music, or a scientist who is compelled to find an answer to a specific scientific question. My mission is simply to inform the world what aromatic plants can do for the body and—since I have discovered their more subtle actions as well—for the spirit. My deepest hope is that this message will help every human being draw closer to his or her Creator and be a better participant in whatever formal religion he or she chooses.

Applications for the Body

Now we will turn to the more physical uses of true lavender essential oil. Do not think our Creator gave it to us only for mental and spiritual reasons. Our Creator endows aromatic plants with a multitude of effects, both spiritual and physical. I began this chapter on a mental/spiritual approach because I feel that true lavender, more than any other essential oil, has a special role to fulfill in the spiritual realm but the purely physical uses are also substantial.

We can group the primary physical benefits of true lavender into three categories: internal purification, burn treatment, and stress relief.

Internal Purification

The word lavender comes from the Latin root word *lavare*, which means to wash. In French the word is *laver*. I am often amazed at the wisdom behind the words we use. Dr. Jean Valnet, MD, a famous French MD who passed away a few years ago, spent his medical career using natural medicine, herbology, and aromatherapy. In his writings, Dr. Valnet listed many properties and indications for essential oils, proposing both internal and external applications. His list for lavender essential oil, particularly the internal uses, is very long, so I will extract just a few, primarily oriented toward the digestive system and its related glands.

Dr. Valnet said of true lavender that it was antibacterial, antiparasitic, and antiseptic. Imagine a pharmaceutical antiseptic designed for external use. To ingest such a substance would be unthinkable. Yet with high grade natural essential oils, as Dr. Valnet explained so well, taking an essential oil internally is not only possible but is often highly advisable. Internal application is a strongly complementary action to topical application. True lavender essential oil activates the secretion of gastric juices and the motility of the intestines. It also increases bile production in the liver and facilitates its secretion through the gall bladder.

We might be able to obtain the same internal response to some degree from external applications, but it is far more efficient to simply ingest a tiny amount. One drop taken internally will have a greater effect than 10 drops applied externally. In Dr. Valnet's time, the most common method of ingesting essential oils was in an alcohol solution. This was fine for a medical doctor, writing a prescription to be filled by a pharmacy. But it is not practical for our everyday personal use. I can give you a much simpler way of taking this essential oil internally, a way that is so easy it can be done anytime with just a moment's preparation.

My method is simply to take an apple and cut it into slices. On a slice of apple, I place a trace of true lavender essential oil and then spread it into the apple slice scratching over the surface with the tines of a fork. The essential oil communicates a gentle scent to the apple. The combination of lavender and apple creates an extraordinary aroma that should be smelled for a few seconds before eating. As it is chewed thoroughly, the essential oil will trigger your taste buds, giving the apple a slightly bitter taste.

As you know, the tongue itself is an important reflex zone. Plants with bitter tastes are known to have a stimulating effect on the liver and the gall bladder. In our modern culture, we are saturated with sugar and extremely sweet tastes; we avoid the bitter like the plague. Yet from an energy medicine perspective, bitter tastes play an important role in maintaining internal balance. Bitter flavors are beginning to become popular in some beverages and salads.

Sugar should be considered more of a drug than a food. It has no nutritive value whatsoever, and robs the cells of rare vitamins and trace elements needed for optimal health. Refined sugar is possibly the major factor in the rise and spread of modern degenerative diseases. Also, an excess of sweet tastes greatly increases mucous in the respiratory system, where it becomes a breeding ground for disease bacteria.

Thus, the bitter taste of lavender essential oil on the tongue gives a benefit Dr. Valnet did not enjoy with his alcohol solutions: a stimulation for the liver and gall bladder, creating better balance in the digestive system. As the apple is chewed, some of the aromatic molecules will be absorbed directly into the bloodstream through the veins under the tongue. The remainder will exert its purifying action inside the stomach, small intestines and colon. This purifying action is accompanied by a feeling of calmness and being in control of yourself.

It is not necessary to eat an apple this way every day. Rather, I suggest that you do this every few days, as you feel the need.

Burn Treatment

It is well to remember the famous accidental discovery of René-Maurice Gattefossé. A French perfume chemist, he accidentally burned his hand while doing lab work and plunged it into a vat of lavender essential oil. His very serious burn healed rapidly with little scarring and no infection. This event triggered the modern day development of medical aromatherapy.

Today, lavender essential oil is well known for its amazing burn healing properties. As long as we are dealing with common first-degree and superficial second-degree burns, true lavender is perhaps the best natural first aid available. Rarely does lavender essential oil create any discomfort and often it relieves much of the pain. It is a wonderful remedy for sunburn, bringing immediate pain relief and often healing the burn in a few hours.

The essential oil should be applied in repeated small traces, gently tapping on and around the burn. Do not expect instantaneous relief. The application should be repeated every minute for the first five minutes; then every five minutes for half an hour. By then you will feel real relief. Keep in mind that, if a source of cold water is available, the first emergency step is to hold the burn area under cold, running water for 10 minutes to draw the 'heat energy' out of the burn.

Stress Relief

We have mentioned before the importance of the area on the back of the neck, and how massaging this area with a diluted essential oil can unblock and release significant amounts of tension. This is particularly true when using true lavender essential oil. In fact, linalool and linalyl acetate have a documented sedative effect that can be helpful at bedtime, in cases of insomnia. Additional massage on the shoulders and on the feet will expand the calming effect and add to overall relaxation.

Daniel's Challenge—the Aromatic Version

My given name is taken from the Old Testament. In the first book of Daniel, we read how the young prophet Daniel was taken prisoner from

Israel to be educated in the king's court in Babylon. Rather than eat the rich meats and wine served to the king's servants, Daniel pleaded for a natural food, referred to as "pulse." He issued a challenge to the king's representative to allow him and his friends to eat "pulse" and water (instead of meat and wine) for 10 days. At the end of the period, the best diet would be determined by the look in their countenances. The challenge was accepted and the proof was in the pudding: pulse and water is healthier than meat and wine.

In the same spirit, I give you another Daniel's challenge—the aromatic version. If you accept this challenge and follow it, you will gently but deeply wash your impurities out of your body, wash bad thoughts and habits from your mind, and wash doubt and fear from your spirit. I challenge you to set aside a week in which to discover the physical and spiritual power of true lavender.

Start on a Monday and begin to do the following four things:

1. Take one drop of true lavender internally each day, using apple slices.
2. Apply a trace of true lavender essential oil under your nose during a 10 minute meditation period each morning, focusing on the kind of person you want to become.
3. Apply one drop in the center of your forehead before sleeping, asking for inspiration and enlightenment.
4. Take some time each day to study a good book, perhaps the Bible, or a book on natural health methods, to facilitate mental clarity and spiritual opening.

Do all of the above every day for five days. On Saturday, carefully schedule at least three hours for a very special event. You will need a partner, ideally your spouse, but if not married, a close trusted friend. This special event is a body massage with diluted true lavender. For lunch, on Saturday, take a few apple slices with the trace of true lavender essential oil; then relax alone for one hour. Then begin the massage. This is ideal for couples because they can reciprocate. The full massage should take another hour. When the massage is complete, remain in a quiet state of deep relaxation for still one more hour. It is during this final one-hour period that the most powerful action of the lavender is felt on the inner recesses of the mind.

If you will do this exercise once a month for three months, you will feel a tangible change and improvement in your mental and spiritual attitudes. Assorted physical problems will likely diminish or disappear, and your feelings about life generally will become more positive. This is real vibrational medicine, and it demonstrates the power of integral aromatherapy in its finest sense.

When following this challenge, to help preserve the transformational effect, do not mix true lavender essential oil with other essential oils. However, when you are using true lavender for its other physical benefits (internal purification, burn treatment or stress relief) it is not only possible but also advisable to blend another essential oil with it to create a synergistic effect.

The essential oil most commonly blended with lavender for therapeutic applications is tea tree. There is a powerful resonance between these two essential oils, and each helps the other act faster and stronger. It is interesting how this mixing affects their aroma and taste. Tea tree's aroma is normally not very pleasant, but when blended with lavender it is modulated to a greater, more pleasant sweetness. Similarly, the taste of true lavender essential oil is normally bitter, but when blended with tea tree essential oil, the taste is modulated to one that is milder and more pleasant. The recommended proportions are one-third true lavender essential oil to two-thirds tea tree essential oil. The tea tree essential oil increases dramatically the antiseptic and antifungal properties of the true lavender essential oil when they are blended.

This blend is very powerful internally. In fact, if you plan to work on internal purification for more than a one-week period, I recommend that you use this blend instead of straight true lavender essential oil. It is an excellent way to begin a purification and restoration program. Remember, however, that any attempt to do internal purification must be accompanied by a program of quality nutrition.

Candidiasis

This lavender/tea tree blend is also very helpful to ladies (and men) who are prone to candidiasis. For this treatment, in addition to a quality nutrition program, you can take one drop of the tea tree/lavender blend each day (1) with some fruit, (2) in some juice, (3) in a honey herbal tea

(4) in some soy yogurt (we try to avoid dairy products) or (5) directly on the tongue, as you prefer. This should be continued without interruption for three weeks. If you use the honey herbal tea, use only natural honey and do not use hot water. Use only lukewarm water.

Remember in any program using essential oils that your mental state is as important as the product you are using. Essential oils cannot be used like allopathic medicines, i.e. unconsciously popping pills. Use thoughts of gratitude as you visualize the action of aromatic molecules bringing purity, balance and joy to your body. Again, life helping life.

Chapter 11: Balsam Fir *(Abies balsamea)*

In France, we have access to hundreds of different essential oils, used extensively in our pharmacies. Medical aromatherapy is an accepted science here.

I should mention, however, that even in France, we cannot assume that all our essential oils are high quality. Only when we meet observe first-hand the actual growing, harvesting, and distillation processes can we really conclude whether a particular essential oil supplier is creating industrial grade or therapeutic grade essential oils. I pride myself in having an extensive knowledge of both good and bad producers, so I can have access to the finest essential oils in the world.

Witnessing the Distillation

Rose-Marie and I were privileged to actually be on-site at the distillery in Quebec, as the very batch of balsam fir essential oil in my kits was produced. It was fascinating to see the small branches of fir needles cut into smaller pieces and then placed into the still. The entire distilling chamber was filled with these branches—many hundreds of pounds of plant material. The chamber was closed and then submitted to the steam process, not for 30 minutes or 1 hour, but for many hours. At the end of the cycle, this huge amount of plant material produced just four liters of precious Canadian balsam fir essential oil. We were satisfied in every way that the quality of this essential oil was second to none.

It has been my special privilege to do in-depth research into the essential oils of all the conifers. It is largely because of this research that I selected, from all the possible conifer essential oils, Canadian balsam fir. Its role is very often as an ingredient in a blend of other oils, because it enhances their effects. It is used in many of my own blends, and I will give you a recipe in this chapter for a powerful respiratory blend with balsam fir essential oil.

Conifers, particularly balsam fir, represent some of the most biologically complex and beautiful trees on our planet. There are fascinating signatures or symbols connected with this magnificent tree that help us recognize its special significance in maintaining health in the body and the mind. In fact, it was conifer essential oils that began to open my eyes to the reality of the psychological and spiritual impact of essential oils generally, in addition to their scientific uses for physical health. Three special experiences, between 1988 and 1991 convinced me that the conifer trees had something very significant to offer the human race. Let me tell you briefly about them.

Three Transformational Experiences

The first occurred while we were in California giving a seminar at the invitation of our friend Kurt Schnaubelt. This was in San Francisco. We wanted to reconnect with our friend and colleague Michael Scholes in Los Angeles. John Steele, who had attended the seminar offered to drive us south along the coastal highway. The scenery was spectacular! As we stopped for the night to eat and sleep, John spoke to us about his research. His interest is much more in the subtle power of essential oils than in the medical side. My position at the time was just the opposite: very involved in the medical, scientific aspects and somewhat skeptical of the intangible side.

He had with him a very special essential oil blend made from several different conifer trees. He wanted us to have an experience with the psychological (subtle) power of essential oils. Just before we retired to sleep, he applied one drop of his special conifer blend on the crown Chakra of both Rose Marie and myself. I had such an incredible night that I will never forget it. It seemed as though my mind was taken into another plane in order to help it grow and develop and progress toward a better, healthier vision of life. Something very unusual had happened to me, and I began from that time to ponder and investigate conifer essential oils more closely.

The second experience occurred two years later in France with a patient named Claire. When she came to me, in February of 1990, she was in the final stages of uterine cancer. The cancer had metastasized and spread to her lungs. She was living in Texas at the time. Her doctors had told her there was nothing she could do but wait for death.

Now I want to be clear about this situation. The only time I practice aromatic medicine on cancer situations is when it is very, very early, or when it is too late for allopathic medicine, and the patient has been abandoned by his/her doctors. Only then is it fair to work exclusively with our natural approach.

Claire flew to France with her husband to see us. As she arrived, I was stunned at her emaciated appearance. She was a walking corpse, nothing but skin and bone, coughing all the time. Her situation was so desperate and yet there she was standing in my office asking for help. I had to do something, even if it would only help in a small way. As I thought about which essential oils to use, I wondered if I shouldn't just pick some of the most delightful aromas to assist her in the dying process. Instead, I chose the opposite. I decided to select the most powerful essential oils I could find in case there was the slightest chance that her body could somehow respond and throw off this terrible disease. Logic and intuition told me it should be a combination of conifer essential oils.

Rose Marie and I treated Claire daily with aromatic sessions using conifer oils. What we witnessed was almost a resurrection. Day after day, Claire came and spent the entire morning with us. It was as if the conifer essential oils somehow transmitted the energy of the sun and the energy of the earth back into the cells of her body. The ceaseless cough tapered off, then stopped. Her appetite returned and she began a strict nutritional diet. Pretty soon she began to gain weight and her will to live returned.

After 30 days of daily aromatic treatments, it was as if she had been reborn. In March of 1990, I gave a lecture on essential oils at a health fair in Paris, and Claire accompanied us and gave her living testimony about her transformation, a transformation that no one could understand or scientifically explain.

The last experience that convinced me of the medical potential of conifer oils—especially for the respiratory system—occurred shortly thereafter. I came in contact with a distiller of conifers located in Le Massif Central, a mountainous region in central France known for its conifers. Mr. C. had been born and raised in these mountains, where the air is pure, free of pollution and filled with the diffusion of pines, firs, and spruces. You would think growing up like this would lead to great respiratory health, but this was not the case for Mr. C. From his youngest years, he had constant problems with ear, nose, and throat infections and bronchitis, apparently due to allergies. For most of his life he had received all the available allopathic medical treatments, but the problems persisted. His condition was still the same when he reached the age of forty, after many years of medical care.

Then his company transferred him to Paris. At this juncture, he decided to quit and start his own distilling company, so he could stay in the mountains. To his credit, he succeeded in this dream and managed to create quite a reasonable business for himself. But the significant point of this story is this: within six months after starting his conifer essential oil distillation business—after working daily with the fragrant vapors of firs and pines—he realized to his great astonishment that his pulmonary and nasal problems has vanished! Gone were the allergies, infections, and coughs. For the first time in 40 years he was able to breathe free.

Living in the pure mountain air surrounded by conifers was not enough. It took six months of working around the concentrated essential oils of those trees to have the desired effect. To me the most significant point of this story is that this healing process involved no medical intervention whatsoever—no doctors, no medication, no pharmacist, no diet change, no psychological counseling. It was solely the power of the conifers that made him a new man.

Production Background

Now let me give you some background for the balsam fir. Many aromatherapy books do not include this essential oil, or if they do, there is very little information. Additionally, therapeutic grade conifer oils are extremely difficult to find, because so much of the plant material is used for other industrial products, such as paper and industrial chemicals.

While teaching a seminar to a group of German-speaking therapists, explaining the critical importance of obtaining very high quality essential oils in order to get good aromatherapy results, one of the attendees asked me about the price of high quality conifer oils. He was taken aback at my answer, explaining that his company routinely purchased conifer oils at prices that were little more than the cost of mineral water! These were high-volume industrial essential oils—considered nothing more than a by-product of the lumber industry—from which are isolated certain chemical compounds, such as alpha-pinene, used as a raw material to prepare synthetic menthol, synthetic Vitamin A, turpentine, and a variety of other chemically-based products. Since these oils are only used to extract one or two components for industrial use, why would industrial companies bother with a careful, slow distillation process to preserve all the therapeutic constituents? The answer is simple—they wouldn't!

The vast commercial market is actually somewhat of an obstacle for us in obtaining therapeutic grade essential oils. This is especially true of the conifer oils. Many producers mix all kinds of species in their distillation—pines, firs and spruces—so you don't really know what oil you have. All commercial distillers use too much heat and pressure to preserve the therapeutic elements of the oils. Dilution and contamination are commonplace. As medical aromatherapy begins to take hold in North America, I am hopeful that more high-grade conifer essential oils will become available. You have the assurance that the Canadian balsam fir essential oil in my kit is the highest quality available, because I personally watched its production

Canadian balsam fir has the Latin name *Abies balsamea.* The meaning of the genus name "Abies" is "living for a long time" or "great longevity." Already we have a tantalizing reason for investigating the fir trees. In French, the name of the fir tree is "sapin" from the Latin root sapientia, meaning "wisdom." So you see, even in its name, we have in the fir tree the "wisdom of the ages." There are two other main groups of conifers beside the Abies genus. They are the genus Pinus (pines) and the genus Picea (spruces).

Canadian balsam fir is only found naturally in North America, primarily in Canada. There are some magnificent fir species in Europe, but not Abies balsamea. It is unique because of the oleoresin called balsam that oozes from its bark. When the bark is cut and collecting tubes placed at the cuts, significant amounts of this oleoresin can be collected. This same process is used on pine trees to collect turpentine resin. The resin from pine trees, however, is very sticky and not at all pleasant to the taste. Balsam is not nearly as thick or sticky and its taste is reasonably pleasant.

Balsam resin has two primary uses. First it is a wound healing substance, used first by the Indians. Second, it is used in the optical industry, because its refraction index is very near that of glass, minimizing image distortion. In these two uses, we see great symbols of the balsam fir tree's mission.

Two Energy Centers

As we did with the other oils, take the lid off your bottle of Canadian balsam fir and hold it about 10" from the nose, allowing the aroma to rise to the nose. Don't bring it close to the nose, especially in the beginning. As its subtle, sweet smell touches your olfactive sensory cells, you realize immediately that there is depth in this aroma that makes you feel you are about to have a profound experience of some kind. Close your eyes and continue breathing this beautiful aroma deeply for a minute or more. When the vial is held away from the nose, you sense that it penetrates the throat and head much the same as the lavender essential oil. But if the vial is held directly under the nose, it seems to center in the throat and heart, just as the geranium essential oil does. In both cases, there is a gentle but firm power in the aroma that communicates peace to the soul. The messages I receive from this essential oil are something like the following:

Everything is all right. Each thing is at its right place in the Universe. Each thing comes in its right time in this world, for all who are open to receive it and prepared to live it.

Gone are old fears, mental blocks and inhibitions. Weakness becomes strength; darkness gives way to light, hesitation changes to calm determination and deep doubts are overpowered by confidence in yourself, in others and in life.

As human beings many of our physical troubles begin or take their source from a psychological issue. We eventually see the physical symptoms, but real and permanent healing must at some point go to the origin of the problem. In this regard, it is possible to do preventive healing on the psyche, acting not to eliminate physical symptoms that have already commenced, but rather to make deep changes in our minds and hearts, such as freely forgiving, eliminating jealousy and envy, and accepting others as they are. It may sound ambitious, but balsam fir essential oil seems especially helpful in doing this preventive mental medicine.

Protection for Health Professionals
This essential oil also has a vital role to play on behalf of health professionals, particularly those involved in natural and wholistic health. One of the issues health professionals know only too well, is the negative energy that can accumulate as they do consultations with several patients each day. Much of their work is in relieving, and, unfortunately, absorbing negative stress. This problem becomes multi-dimensional in that this stress or negative energy can be transmitted back to other patients, or taken home where it transfers to family members.

As you know by now, I circulate freely among two circles of aromatherapy, both those involved in hard science and those who focus on the more subtle, psychological effects. In a meeting of the latter group, when discussing the problem of negative transfer, one professional offered that he had eliminated much of the problem by using balsam fir essential oil. It was agreed the entire group would participate in an informal clinical exercise to test this suggestion. To our surprise, it was confirmed by all who participated that balsam fir essential oil created tangible protection against negative transfer.

How can you use it for this purpose?

1. Before leaving for work, apply one drop of balsam fir essential oil to the kidney one point (roughly at the reflex point for the solar plexus) on each foot.
2. Apply a trace of the essential oil on the forehead, on the nape of the neck, on the sternum or on the top of the head before seeing each new patient and before going home.

Sensitive therapists will easily feel the vibrational protective action of the balsam fir essential oil.
The therapists in Europe strongly agreed that, at the end of the workday, they felt better and stronger when they used this essential oil. We are speaking here of clinical observations. Even hard science has to start from observations.

I would like North American therapists to do this same experiment. Apply this same technique in your practice every day for at least four weeks and report your findings. Of course, it is critical here that you have access to and use a high quality balsam fir essential oil. If you use a low grade/adulterated tea tree essential oil for a sore throat and then find that the tea tree does not work, it is not the fault of tea tree essential oil, but rather the problem of poor quality. Report your results through Essentia, c/o Therapy Project, PO Box 50525, Provo, UT 84605

Two Blends for Respiratory Relief

Balsam fir essential oil demonstrates its most powerful effect when used in a synergistic way as part of a blend. And what essential oil would blend especially well with it? Eucalyptus radiata, of course, is the staple essential oil for use in pulmonary congestion. The eucalyptus is surrounded with the gentleness and staying power of the balsam fir; and the balsam fir seems to acquire an extra degree of strength from the eucalyptus. When you mix these two essential oils for respiratory purposes, use the following proportion:

3 drops of eucalyptus essential oil
1 drops of balsam fir essential oil

The combination of these two oils is synergistic. Their combined total action is greater than the sum of their parts. Instead of 6 + 2 = 8 action units, we get 6 x 2 = 12 action units. You can enhance this respiratory blend even further by combining it with the earlier blend mixed from tea tree and lavender. Mix the blend according in these proportions:

6 drops eucalyptus essential oil
2 drops balsam fir essential oil
6 drops tea tree essential oil
3 drops true lavender essential oil

This blend adds the extra anti-infectious power of tea tree and the anti-spasmodic (anti-cough) characteristic of lavender to the respiratory clearing powers of eucalyptus and balsam fir.

Balsam Fir Relaxation Session

Lastly, let me describe to you a wonderful application that I call the balsam fir oil assisted relaxation session. This is usually best done in the evening, although some people may find that balsam fir makes it hard to go to sleep. Each person will have to test himself/herself on this point. The great advantage of evening application is the potential for very deep work taking place in the subconscious during sleep and dreams.

One caution should be raised here. Particularly in cases where large amounts of negative stress and negative energy have accumulated over long periods of time, dreams may occur that will be more like nightmares than sweet inspirations! This is a normal elimination process. Soon there will be a change in the content of your dreams, and they will be filled with positive nighttime inspirations.

The relaxation session will take at least 30 minutes. It is a mental cleansing and purification technique that should be done in a quiet, dark room on a bed or couch. Simply use a dropper to place one drop of balsam fir essential oil on the center of the forehead (the third eye Chakra). Do not touch this drop with your fingers. Instead allow it to just stay there and absorb spontaneously into the skin.

You will experience a slow energy and information transfusion process. Your body controls the speed at which this takes place, so don't try to rush it. The typical sequence of events is as follows:

1. During the first 5-10 minutes, the beginning process of normal relaxation occurs. The usual sensations of increased calmness and relaxation are felt with no real noticeable aromatic effects.
2. After about 10 minutes a significantly different feeling begins. The relaxation becomes deeper. The feeling is that the mind is being penetrated and purified, changing the way the world is perceived. There is an impression that old mental baggage is being set outside.
3. A completely relaxing letting-go process seems to occur with out argument or resistance. It is accomplished without a strug gle, without an effort.

This last characteristic is the most unusual about this experience. Typically, when we encounter the need to let go of old, unhelpful mental patterns, they do not go without a fight. Even when we know these patterns are wrong and detrimental, our conscious mind wants to hang on to them, because they are mental habits. The greater mental clarity that is achieved with the help of balsam fir essential oil makes it easier to walk away from these bad habits.

If you finally understand that your wounds are actually self-inflicted, because of the way you think and perceive, you begin to realize that these wounds cannot go away until your own thinking changes. If this relaxation with balsam fir oil is practiced regularly over time, accompanied by some psychological support, major changes may occur in your behavior.

When the aromatic relaxation session is over, there is a feeling of living as a new person in a new world. Events and people that used to trigger defensive reactions or rejection can now be perceived with a level of detachment. They become integrated into a broader perspective of having some positive purpose in the grand scheme of things.

Chronic Nasal Catarrh and Chronic Sinusitis

A problem that bothers millions of Americans and Europeans is sinusitis. It involves chronic inflammation/infection of the sinuses and chronic catarrh in the back of the nose. The problem is so common in industrialized societies that most people don't even realize they have an infection! Yet, when I test for it, touching a reflex point on each side of the upper nose, slightly inward and upward from the inner corner of the eye, 90-95% of my patients feel significant tenderness, indicating a problem.

I presented considerable information and several techniques for helping this problem in *Natural Home Health Care Using Essential Oils.* Anyone with a particular interest in addressing this problem in a thorough way should refer to that book also.

Here I will present some simple techniques that can be used with balsam fir essential oil. Its special characteristic is its unusual gentleness. The skin areas around the eyes and sinuses are very sensitive, and balsam fir is one of the few essential oils that can be applied neat in trace amounts near these areas. Of course, those with allergies must still be very careful in this application.

The treatment is performed by placing a trace of diluted balsam fir essential oil on each forefinger and, beginning at the outside end of the eyebrow, massaging very gently just under the eyebrow toward the top of the nose. **You must be extremely careful doing this, to insure that no trace gets in the eye.** As your fingers move closer and closer to the center of the face, along the eyebrow, you will reach the above-mentioned sinus reflex point (which I call the "ouch point," because so many people feel soreness here.) It is located on the side and at the very top of the nose, just under the eyebrow. The more tender this spot feels, the gentler you should massage. Tenderness on this point is not a normal condition. It is an indication of a chronic condition in the sinuses that is probably years or even decades old. I assure you that after a proper treatment program, this tenderness does disappear. Antibiotics will tend to keep this problem going for years, pushing it deeper inside, sometimes making it worse.

A second application point for sinusitis with balsam fir is the fontanelle point. Apply one drop of neat essential oil with the little finger.

A third point was described by Dr. T. Jeanneau a French MD, who did research to relate one hundred and fifty different essential oils to specific acupuncture points. His work was presented at the 1998 Grasse (France) *Symposium on Integrated Aromatic Medicine* (proceedings available from Essential Science Publishing, 800-336-6308). Balsam fir essential oil was related to what is known at the 64th point of the bladder meridian. This is located on the outside of the foot. You can find it by tracing with your finger from the fifth toe, along its connecting bones toward the heel. The point is about 1/2" in from the base of the little toe, at the joint of the connecting metatarsal bone. Apply a half-drop of balsam fir essential oil on each foot at these points. Chinese medicine specifies several indications connected to this point, including one that is highly relevant, namely, chronic nasal catarrh. Catarrh is an inflammation of mucous membranes, usually resulting in additional secretion of mucous. The connection to sinusitis is not coincidental.

Muscular/Skeletal Toning

Balsam fir does not stop acute pain, like peppermint can, but it can be very helpful to the joints and muscles through regular massage. Particularly for degenerative conditions and sore muscles, balsam fir essential oil works very deeply, not like a pain-killing analgesic to relieve symptoms, but with a toning and strengthening influence that helps the body heal. Because of its gentleness, balsam fir can be applied neat to smaller joints and muscles for its most powerful effect. If massage is required, dilute 10-15 drops of essential oil in 10 ml of carrier oil. This should be used to massage the larger joints and muscles and along the spine and back.

Chapter 12: Lemon *(Citrus limon)*

Now we travel to Sicily to begin our discussion of lemon. The choice of Sicilian fruit is simple—it provides fruit of top research quality. Sicilian distillers start exclusively from certified (Ecocert) organically grown fruits, and produce both organic orange and lemon essences. This is significantly different from growers in North and South America who regularly spray heavy pesticides, insecticides and fertilizers. The fruit peel, the very place we go to obtain citrus essence, absorbs these chemicals.

Lemon (as well as other citrus essences) is different from herbal essential oils in that it is obtained through a process of cold pressing, rather than steam-distillation. The fruit peel is mechanically pressed, yielding what is correctly termed, "lemon peel essence." Some experts argue that the heat from steam distillation affects the chemical structure of the resulting essential oil. Lemon essence is obtained directly, without having to undergo any heat or steam exposure from distillation. Hence the use of the term "essence" instead of "essential oil." Lemon essence can be steam-distilled like other essential oils, but the distillation process when applied to citrus fruits yields only the essential oil, not the more powerful, more pungent, pure essence.

We are rightly concerned with the purity of the essence, and the raw materials that are used to make the essence, because inevitably, the purity and quality of the essence will affect its overall power and efficacy. The Japanese diffuse a chemical, reminiscent of the lemon scent into factories and offices to improve the work environment and enhance worker productivity and accuracy. However, in using a cheaper, synthetic industrial counterfeit, they are expecting results without using the real remedy. Experience has shown repeatedly that we must work with the highest-grade materials when we work with essential oils.

Perhaps the most identifiable characteristic of the lemon is its scent. From a purely olfactive or aesthetic point of view, the lemon scent is universally recognized and appreciated by cultures all over the world. If you present a piece of strong French cheese to the Chinese, they may be repelled and disgusted by its aroma. Conversely, in China and southern Asia, there is a fruit eaten that, to our Western sense of smell, appears extremely offensive and obnoxious. The scent of lemon, however, transcends all cultural boundaries. Lemon scent is even enjoyed by our five dogs, who sometimes flee at the sight of a vial of essential oil!

Because lemon is a universally-enjoyed scent, we must recognize its ability to universally dynamize, energize, and accelerate the following five areas:

- Purification of the body
- Clarification of the mind
- Opening of the heart
- Harmonization of the soul
- Elevation of the spirit

I selected for my singles kit, essential oils that would provide maximum benefit with a minimum number of relatively economical but very high quality oils. This approach is quite different from other companies who may encourage you to purchase a great number of oils of lesser quality and benefits. Our greatest desire is to help you make the most of a few high quality, affordable essential oils.

Today we think that when we are ill, all we have to do is "take a pill" and the medicine will do the work for us. Rarely does this approach deal with the real causes of the problem, particularly the mental or emotional causes. The special benefit of essential oils is that they work in physical and psychological ways at the same time.

For many, citrus oils also have a spiritual application. For the Greeks, the garden of the Hesperides was their picture of Paradise. The "Hesperides" is also a collective name given to the different varieties of citrus fruits.

Citrus essences

Lemon essence can be used in both practical physiological and psychological applications. It can be taken internally or used topically.

Whenever intellectual or mentally creative work is required, lemon essence is very helpful. It stimulates the mind in these endeavors. As I sat down to write about lemon essence and its wholistic power, I brought a drop of lemon essence close to my nose and inhaled. I immediately yawned in a deep and easy way—a sign that my brain was ready to work with ideas. I applied one small drop on the fontanelle point, above my forehead, and a trace at my nostrils. I then began typing, and as I received the ideas, sentences and words came to my mind one after another. Sometimes the material came so fast my fingers could hardly work quickly enough!

For practical applications, Dr. Valnet indicates that lemon is a diuretic and decongestant of the liver. For treating hay fever, I have used lemon essence with the application of colored rays, using the yellow wavelengths to bring cold and dryness whenever there was an acute excess of fluid and heat.

In a wholistic weight-loss program, lemon and grapefruit essences can help stimulate the elimination organs of the body. The psychological effects of lemon can help the overweight person better select the appropriate foods and exercise self-control in the face of temptation.

Topical application

Lemon essence can be applied topically; however, you should never apply a drop directly on the forehead if it will be exposed to direct sunlight. It should be applied on the anterior fontanelle (the area of the head where you would find a baby's soft spot). Lemon also has an upper affinity with the sixth chakra on the forehead. This is mainly from breathing it and applying it on the fontanelle area.

When using lemon essence topically, you must be aware of the consequences of photosensitization. As a general rule with cold-pressed essences, you should exercise caution when applying citrus essences topically and then exposing the applied area to direct sunlight. Suppose you apply a few drops on your left forearm and then go into the sun with your forearm exposed, there is a high risk that a brown mark will form where the essence was applied, similar to exposing your arm to a UV lamp. This is due to the coumarins that are extracted by the cold-expression process. If the lemons were steam-distilled, there would be no risk, because the coumarins are destroyed by heat. However, then you would not have the benefits of the raw essence! These coumarins, present only in the raw essence, have been shown to have a calming effect on the nervous system, and a positive impact on the circulatory system, including thinning the blood and increasing the resistance of the capillaries.

If you apply lemon essence on an exposed part of your body, wait 24 hours before spending time in the direct sunlight.

Internal application

When lemon essence is taken internally, its elective area of action is the third chakra and the related organs, chiefly the stomach, liver, gall bladder, pancreas, and spleen. The kidneys and adrenal glands can also be affected.

For an internal lemon drink, try this morning recipe. First, purchase some organic lemons. For those who live in the southern part of the country, you can easily get them in local gardens. If not, you can find them in organic shops.

In an 8-oz. glass, press a teaspoon of juice from a fresh lemon. Add to the juice one drop of organic lemon essence and stir them together. Add pure water and stir the liquid clockwise for 15 seconds in order to activate the essence mixture and the water. When you stir the water and essence mixture, remember that it should be more than a mechanical or automatic gesture. Accompany it with uplifting thoughts.

When you're ready to swallow, always drink small amounts at a time, letting the liquid remain in your mouth for a few seconds. Though the drink may taste sour and slightly bitter, it is important not to add sugar to your aromatic whole-lemon drink.

If you were to try the same recipe *without* the lemon essence, you would find the taste to be much more acidic. The lemon essence buffers the sour taste of the lemon juice.

It is important to drink this lemon drink at the right time. If you drink it in the morning when you wake up, you should not immediately have your breakfast. Wait at least 15 minutes after drinking, giving it time to leave the stomach. If you wish to drink it later, after a meal, wait two to three hours, depending on what you ate. If you had lipids such as oil or butter, wait four hours before drinking it.

You will find that drinking this aromatic whole lemon beverage regularly helps to create a strong action throughout your body, and you will see the difference in many ways, even on your skin.

For the ultimate lemon challenge, drink five to six glasses of lemon drink during the morning, from the moment you wake up until one hour before lunch. Then have a healthy lunch at 1 p.m. This is an excellent way to cleanse the liver and gall bladder as well as the kidneys. For those following a weight control program, this will boost the "fat burning" processes and aid in the body's elimination of dead matter in the tissues. Research has shown that the use of lemon in the body may also aid in the prevention of cancer.

You can also add a drop of lemon essence to any dessert or drink. After using the juice of the organic lemon, you can grate the rind and add it to any culinary preparation. You can always follow the classic herbal tea recipe by adding warm water to a drop of essence dissolved in honey. The grated peel itself can also be added to the classic herbal tea recipe.

The following experience illustrates one important use of lemon essence.

> Some parents drove from Paris to our house (about 390 miles) to have me look at their 7-year old daughter who had Downs Syndrome. The purpose was not to treat the chromosomal condition itself, but to help them in their decision to stop the constant antibiotic treatments that she was receiving year-round for throat and lung infections. Though these conditions are common in most children, it was especially severe for this child. Rose-Marie explained to the parents the necessity of changing her diet and prescribed healthy nutritional recipes that would work hand-in-hand with aromatic treatments. I taught them when, how, and why to use essential oils in both a daily preventative way and intensively as a response to infection. We showed the parents how to stimulate major reflex areas on their daughter's feet, and gave them three vials of blends to use—one on the thorax and feet, another along her neck, and a special synergy for internal use. Just before leaving, they asked, "By the way, Dr. Penoel, her 4-year old brother is always sick in the car. He feels nauseous and often vomits. Do you have anything in your oils that could help him?"

> Although peppermint is usually a first choice, this is more appropriate for adults and older children. For a very young child, the best choice is lemon essence. I provided them with a 10-ml vial of lemon essence and directed them to put a drop on a handkerchief or tissue and crumple it, making sure the spot of oil did not directly touch the nose or face. I instructed them to have the child breathe through the aromatic handkerchief as soon as he enters the car, and repeat this "lemon essence breathing" as often as required. The parents did as I directed and the boy was never sick again. And by the way, the daughter never took any more antibiotics!

Lemon essence can help the nausea and vomiting problem in many instances apart from young children. Pregnant women with morning sickness have found relief by taking two drops in the morning with some honey (a lump of sugar is not the best choice, but may be accepted).

Creating a Lemon-based Essential Oil Blend

You can use two oils in my kit to create a powerful essential oil blend. Tea tree oil and lemon essence both have a strong affinity for the solar plexus chakra, and may be used to create what I call a "horizontal" synergy between both of them. When creating oil/essence blends, we must pay close attention to the proportions of the different ingredients. To create the synergy, begin by putting eight drops of tea tree oil in a small vial. Take time to smell the tea tree oil, so you may be able to accurately perceive the correct proportion once the lemon essence is added. Begin adding drops of lemon essence, one by one, inhaling the synergy as you do until you perceive that the correct proportions have been reached. In my research, I have found that a ratio of approximately 5 drops of lemon essence to 8 drops of tea tree oil is the average correct proportion.

This blend can be taken internally in the same way as the lemon essence, and will exert a powerful action on the entire digestive system. The tea tree essential oil provides a cleansing action extended into the lower part of the digestive system. The effects of the synergy on the immune system are far greater than the benefits of each isolated product.

Diluted in a carrier oil, this blend can be used for massage in the solar plexus area, and is also useful for massaging the joints in cases of degenerative rheumatism. Applying the blend to the kidney area stimulates elimination and activates the adrenal glands. The blend may also be applied to the spleen, liver, and thymus areas.

Please remember that lemon essence is more fragile than other essential oils. It can get easily become oxidized, especially because of heat. It is best to keep your vial in the refrigerator so that you do not loose any of its great effectiveness.

I remind you that, in our wholistic aromatic method, it is indispensable to work with single essential oils on the one hand *and* with blends on the other hand. A product of the first category does not replace a product of the second.

Chapter 13 : Introduction to Blends

It is a joy to introduce these first five blends. We have started a development program that will—in time—bring to the marketplace a total of 12 basic blends. The first five constitute the first of two blends kits. There will be seven more in a second kit. Before presenting each blend in depth, I would like to introduce a few ideas about essential oils in blended forumulae.

First of all, there is no 'either/or' decision to be made between single oils and blends. Having access to excellent quality single essential oils does not preclude us from working with blends. Using powerful blends does not imply that we should abandon, discontinue or become skeptical about using single essential oils. We work regularly with both to take full advantage of all the potentials inherent in essential oils.

The blends can accomplish things that no single essential oil could do; yet the single oils have potentials that cannot be replaced by a blend. You should consider single essential oils to be the creative work of Nature. Blends on the other hand, involve creative work both by Nature and by Man.

Formulating a specific blend, as you will see, can be at the same time both very scientific and very artistic. On the one hand, the formulator may select essential oils based on their chemical constituents, assemble a logical group of molecules known to have specific effects on the body. On the other hand, essential oils are so complex in their make-up and interactions that the formulator may not be able to predict with certainty exactly how the final blend will perform. Neither will he or she know for certain, before the blend is mixed, exactly what its aroma will be, if that is a consideration. The proof, as they say, is in the pudding.

Remember that each single essential oil may have a hundred or more identifiable constituents. I emphasize "identifiable" because we know there are many more molecules in essential oils that have not yet even been identified. Hundreds are being discovered each year! So essential oil chemistry is not an exact science. We deal with approximations and likelihoods in most cases.

The fascinating part of essential oil blends is the uniqueness inherent in each formula. You will find that each formulator has his or her own characteristics in the blends they create. It has to do with the types and quality of single oils they combine and also with the whole purpose for the resulting blend. I take much pride in the blend formulae I have created. Many have told me that my blends have a special effect that others do not.

There are many different reasons why blends are created. In my medical practice, I regularly create specific blends for specific patients, based solely on their unique needs and problems. In creating these blends, I frequently use as many as 20 or 30 different essential oils! I refer to these as Level II blends because of the number of ingredient oils and their sometimes complex application protocols.

I refer to the blends in these two blends kits as Level I blends. They are practical and reasonably affordable, while still being very powerful. They are easy to use and usually consist of 5 to 10 ingredient oils.

In the perfume industry, there are many exotic combinations of essential oils, usually supplemented with various synthetic chemicals and absolutes, since the aroma is the sole concern. By contrast, in medicine, we sometimes create blends with aromas that are a bit unpleasant, yet we use them anyway because of their specific therapeutic potential. Some blends are created to have an aggressive action on certain bacteria or viruses. Others are created to have a gentle harmonizing effect on body systems. Still others may be created to have a stimulating effect on certain systems or feelings.

My primary purpose in blending essential oils has always been for medical purposes. In more recent years, I have become more sensitive to the potential for psychological or "subtle" effect from blends. With my wife's help, I have developed some appreciation for the therapeutic effects of very well developed aromas that are focused on the olfactive sense. In creating therapeutic blends, however, the overriding goals are to make a substance that will be (1) safe, (2) effective, (3) easier to use than single oils, and (4) synergistically focused in that a small amount will create a powerful specific effect. A final goal is to (5) make the aroma of the blend at least tolerable and, ideally, utterly delightful.

These five blends were created with some very specific actions in mind. I chose five fundamental objectives that would make them foundation blends in any household.

1. A respiratory blend to combine every positive action in several single oils to strengthen and clear the pulmonary and nasal systems
2. A defense blend, designed to prevent and eliminate potential infections
3. An exercise blend, with specific molecules to support the muscles and the joints
4. A calming blend to powerfully relieve physical and mental stress
5. An intimacy blend to combine olfactive ecstasy while heightening the other senses.

Chapter 14: The Respiratory Blend

In writing about the blends, one of my goals is to help you understand how the body functions and how the aromatic molecules help the body activate those functions. Because our approach is a wholistic one, we know that breathing is more than a physiological process. Learning to control our breathing can be a major help in controlling some of our emotions.

The Digestive-Respiratory Connection:
The first two years of medical school are devoted to learning the structure and the functions of the normal human body. The next four years are devoted to studying the various diseases. Official medicine never seems to establish a logical link between the two. This problem is almost schizophrenic!

The simple truth behind this split attitude is simply that it produces doctors to rarely have to ask their patients to change their lifestyle. In fact, if you really want to stay healthy, you need to consult a "health specialist" instead of a doctor, who is more of a "disease specialist." Medical doctors never receive complete training in health. Their primary concern is disease. The sad and persistent consequence of this attitude is the prescribing of allopathic drugs, which are supposed to cure the disease. This arrangement insures that companies who patent synthetic compounds for prescription drugs will have a thriving business for a long time to come.

One fact that most medical doctors miss is the intimate connection between digestive health and respiratory health.

First of all, we know that it is vital for the entire respiratory system to be, in a way, lubricated. This enables the gaseous function of the lungs to let in oxygen and let out carbon dioxide. The lungs receive an intense blood supply on the one hand and a lymphatic supply from a vessel called the thoracic duct on the other.

All the lipids (fats and oils) that you eat eventually arrive in the lungs. If they are in excess, specialized cells engulf the particles and your secretions carry them out of the body. The most tempting foods of our day contain the heaviest lipids. And they have the most dangerous effect on your respiratory system. Butter, cheese, cream and all fatty dairy products—chocolate, ice creams, and rich deserts are heavy in lipids and are sadly the most common foods in an American or a French diet. Most oils are used in the modern Western diet are totally dead, because they are processed by solvent extraction and heat. There are healthier choices, and it is your responsibility to learn about them and change your nutritional pattern.

Let me illustrate with the following cases.

A woman in her thirties consulted me for a very severe case of asthma. Her condition had lasted for many years and was getting worse despite all medical treatments. Not one doctor had taken the time to ask about her nutritional habits. By looking at her (she was very thin) you would never imagine that her diet was completely wrong. But I make it a point to ask about lifestyle and nutrition.

As you know eating is more than feeding your cells! It is often a way to compensate for a psychological emptiness in your life. In her case she was from Northern Europe and was married to a French engineer who had to travel all the time. She felt very lonely and to compensate for her loneliness, she ate little pieces of cheese all day long in such a compulsive way that it represented a large amount of heavy animal fat that ended up being evacuated into the pulmonary alveoles and became stagnant in the bronchial ducts. Her asthma was primarily the result of this excess animal fat. But an even deeper origin of her asthma was in the psychological realm. In such cases, if you do not tackle the problem at its origin (the psyche), you cannot solve it by imposing a healthy diet, because it will not be followed.

When I explained to her what she would have to change in her lifestyle in order to improve her condition, she replied that she was not willing to change anything. At least, her answer was an honest one. And it was the end of my consultation.

Matiette was another patient who came to me when she was in her seventies. She was accompanied by her mother in her nineties, who was very worried about her daughter's health!

Matiette had been sick with the flu and her doctor had prescribed antibiotics (which is futile in most cases, since they do not attack viruses). The flu itself ended as it always does, but Mariette kept a permanent irritation in her lungs and her bronchial system. She was coughing all the time and was not able to evacuate the glue-like mucous that seemed to be blocked deep inside her lungs. It was as though the normal process of maturation and evacuation that accompanies a bronchial infection had been arrested by the antibiotics. And since that time, everything was buried inside her. Mariette had lost a lot of weight because of this permanent lung irritation. So when she came to me a year later, she weighed very little! It is probably for this reason that I started the aromatic treatment without checking her diet. For several months I used essential oils with good progress. Yet, it seemed that the treatment came very close to the threshold of the healing, and then she again would fall back in a new and more difficult phase.

For Mariette, it took three major changes to bring about her full healing. First, my wife thoroughly reviewed her food intake and found many vital errors. She was particularly fond of butter on white bread, which is very mucous forming because the starch makes glue in the lungs, a real danger in her situation. The second key was her aromatic treatment. I used aerosol sessions with high tech devices using a special essential oil called inula. It is indeed an extremely expensive essential oil, but tiny amounts can give excellent results. In her case, a single aerosol session with inula triggered an impressive reaction. She expelled packets of thick mucous that had been kept very deep inside her bronchial tree! The third factor that played a large role was the decision to put her under a permanent directional aerosol or unheated diffusing system throughout the night, so that we could take advantage of her sleeping hours for breathing aromatic particles.

With this completely balanced approach, changes did not take long. Within three weeks, she was breathing normally, and after a few months she had regained her normal weight and was completely healed.

Preventing Mucous Congestion

By combining a nutritional diet and essential oils, you receive a synergistic healing effect. Overall health can improve many times over what it would be with only one or the other. Let's say that by changing your diet alone you reach an improvement level of six. And using specific essential oils or a specialized blend you reach a five on the same scale. If you combine both nutritional correction and essential oils, you do not get 5 + 6 = 11 but rather 5 x 6 = 30.

To stay alive, we need oxygen. We also need to eat. It is impossible to have good absorption of oxygen and efficient elimination of carbon dioxide, if the respiratory system is covered with thick mucous. Do you think that your car will work properly and burn the fuel you put in it if the air filter is completely clogged? How do you prevent this? Well, first of all, you need to use a high quality gasoline. This is the equivalent of good nutrition. If the air filter is clogged, you must clean it. Nature supplies us with the substances that will help keep our respiratory systems free of deposits.

We have three categories of aromatic molecules we can use. If I ask you where your respiratory system is gently stimulated, you might answer, "in a pine or fir tree forest." Someone who lives in Australia would answer, "in a forest of eucalyptus trees." So we extract the concentrated aromatic substance from the needles of the conifers and from the leaves of the "gum tree"(a common name for the Australian Eucalyptus). These essences can be combined into a convenient essential oil blend. Their purpose, from a molecular point of view, is to reinforce the power of the molecule of cineole (contained in *Eucalyptus radiata*) with the monoterpenes of the **balsam fir.**

The respiratory blend I created is a "horizontal synergy," in the sense that the power of the Australian ***Eucalyptus radiata*** is reinforced with the power of essential oil extracted from the leaves of a tree called **niaouli** that grows in Madagascar. The concept of horizontal synergy means that both eucalyptus and niaouli contain the same molecule—cineole. What is the interest of niaouli? Well, we all know that allergies are becoming widespread, especially respiratory allergies. Air pollution plays a big role, but keep in mind that even the pollution in foods and eating wrong foods contributes to respiratory allergic manifestations. Niaouli essential oil contains molecules that help relieve and prevent respiratory allergies. In a general purpose blend, it is wise to include it as a complement to *Eucalyptus radiata*. It would be wrong for you to suppose that niaouli essential oil is redundant since there is already eucalyptus. Redundancy does not apply to the world of aromatic plants!

With *Eucalyptus radiata*, niaouli and balsam fir, we have a powerful synergy for making the mucous more fluid and decreasing possible allergic reactions. Using this basic aromatic blend, you receive benefits from three diverse countries—Canada, Madagascar, and Australia—in the form of the essential oils of their best trees, carefully selected for your respiratory system!

But there is more.

The Natural Dissolving Power of Specific Molecules

Making the mucous more fluid is an initial step in creating the best possible blend for the respiratory system. Believe me, modern medicine has been extremely ineffective in this effort! The other advantage of the aromatic molecules in this blend is, if used regularly, they provide great preventative protection. The blend creates thinner mucus and regulates its secretion. But when the glue-like mucous is blocked inside, even stronger molecules are required.

Women remove their nail polish with a chemical called acetone. It is very strong and obnoxious smelling. But nature, in its generosity, provides us with aromatic molecules that possess the ketone function, a strong dissolving action, and yet they are not at all obnoxious, as is acetone. We call them monoterpenic ketones.

In our respiratory blend, we use the essential oils of four more aromatic plants—peppermint, spearmint, caraway and *Eucalyptus dives*. **Peppermint** contains, besides menthol, the corresponding ketone molecule called menthone. **Spearmint** and **caraway** contain a ketone molecule named carvone. ***Eucalyptus dives*** contains a ketone molecule called piperitone.

It is important to keep in mind that we do not separate these molecules (as the pharmaceutical industry would do, thus eliminating many other naturally supporting molecules), but we use them as we obtain them from Nature through steam distillation of the leaves of the plant.

Identifying an active component does not mean that other ingredients are not important. For instance, in *Eucalyptus dives*, there are several alcohols, chiefly piperitol, with interesting anti-infectious properties.

When the four ketone-rich essential oils are combined together we have created another horizontal synergy. It is this powerful synergy that plays a major role in dissolving the glue-like mucous. When this synergy is combined with the balasm fir, *Eucalyptus radiata* and niaouli synergy, we now have a double blend with the power to both dissolve mucous and also make it more fluid. No pharmaceutical company could create such a logical and scientifically conceived blend with such a strong power and a nice scent!

Learning to Use Your Respiratory Blend

This blend is quite strong. I am not saying that it irritates the skin. Of course, if you are prone to allergies, you will be extra careful. The strength I refer to has to do with the complexity of the blend and the power that it acquires through multiple synergies between its components.

Its first function is to keep the mucous membrane of the respiratory system fairly clean. The respiratory blend can and should be used externally as well as internally, in order to obtain the best results. Just remember the intestinal/lung connection and that cleansing the lungs begins by cleansing the digestive system. If the septic tank is clogged, the atmosphere in the bathroom will soon become very unpleasant! Just spraying some air freshener will cover up the unpleasant odors for a while, but the tank needs to be emptied and the flow reestablished. This applies to the human body. Healthy nutrition and regular use of aromatic compounds are the two necessary conditions for keeping it as clean as possible.

There are several ways to use the respiratory blend for acute conditions and chronic conditions. It should be used regularly, especially for prevention. Use it whenever you feel the need to clear your respiratory system, especially during the cold and flu season. You should normally avoid peppermint just before bed. However, peppermint is accompanied by so many other essential oils in this blend that you can use it at night without effecting your sleep (although each individual should test this effect to be sure.)

Even in an intense condition the amount used in each application is still the same—use a small amount at a time but repeat the application every few minutes. Decrease application frequency as symptoms subside.

External Applications with the Respiratory Blend
When the blend is used on small specific areas, apply a small drop at a time. Here is a list of specific areas for neat application of a small drop:

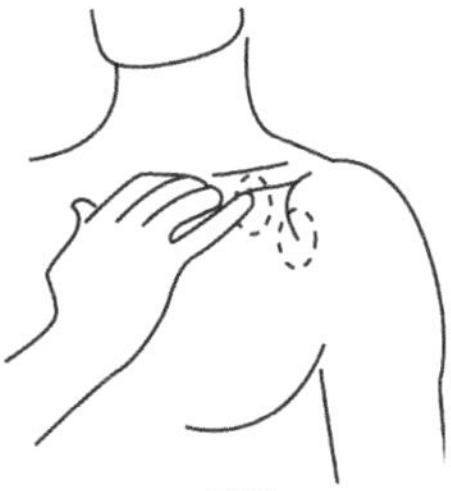

- below the outer area of the clavicle (collar bone) and just inside the groove between the deltoid and the pectoralis major muscles (These are first and second points of the lung meridian)
- upper part of the sternum
- on the groove of the radial pulse on the wrist
- on the extremities of the fingers, just under the nail
- just under the toenails
- on the lung area of the feet (the ball of the foot)
- on the control points of the lung meridian—on each side of the spine, under the third dorsal vertebra
- on each side of the nostril (just a trace)
- on the anterior fontanelle (the area of the soft spot on a baby's head)
- on the bone behind the ear and under the ear

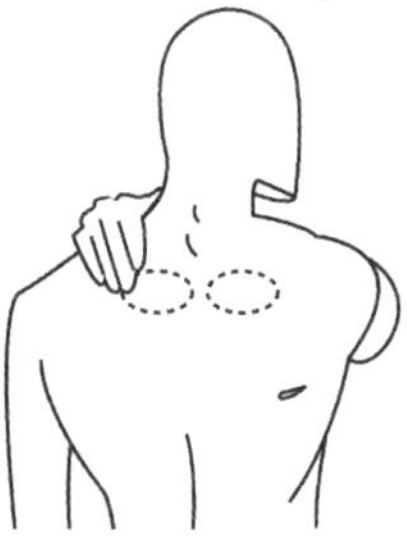

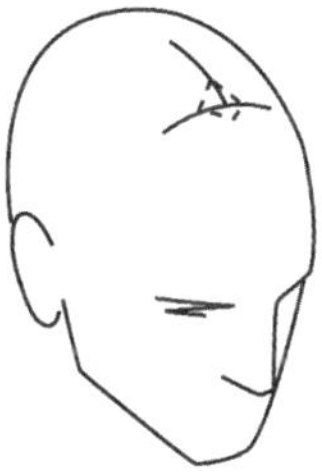

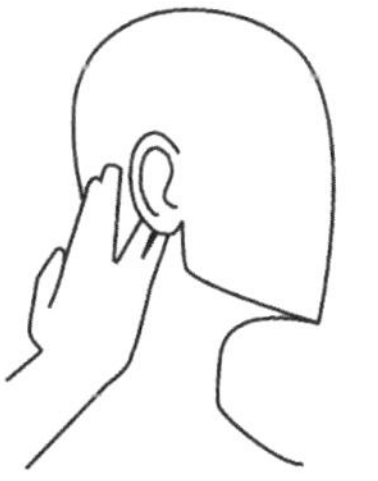

These spots are connected neurologically with acupuncture meridians/points and reflex areas, or are connected by anatomical relationships.

Remember that essential oils are perfectly suited to become part of your regular daily hygiene! This is the only way for you to reap the benefits of improved health and vitality over the long run.

Some Examples of External Applications
When you use an undiluted drop of the respiratory blend, or any of the other non-irritating essential oils, you will feel them absorb quickly and

diffuse through your body. Never rub the essential oils into your skin as you would a lotion. Carefully apply the drop with the dropper and spread the oil gently on the specified area with your fingertips without rubbing. If you wish to massage, blend five drops of the respiratory blend in one tablespoon of the carrier oil. That should be enough for a whole session.

A patient of mine had an infection in her nose and sinuses, which she thought she was over until she realized that the hearing in her left ear had decreased dramatically. Because of her recent infection, I suspected the middle ear behind the eardrum must have become clogged with mucous. As you know there is a thin channel called the Eustachian tube that connects the pharynx with the middle ear. It was likely that the same secretions that had accumulated in the nose, the pharynx, and the sinuses had invaded the middle ear through this tube. I gave her a program to follow at home. I recommended that each hour she use a drop of the respiratory blend. She faithfully applied one drop ten to twelve times a day just behind, under and a little in front of the ear. About two weeks after beginning this aromatic care, her daughter called her, and she put the receiver to her impaired ear and was amazed to be able to hear again!

If you decide to follow a program of respiratory purification using the respiratory blend, you can apply it on several different areas and rotate them at each application. If this is done two or three times a day over one to two weeks, you will see noticeable improvement. It will usually be felt first and most clearly in the nostrils but soon it will even change the way you breathe. The area most directly connected with the nose and sinuses is the anterior fontanelle. One or two drops applied here can have a profound action in clearing thick secretions from your sinus cavities. Those of you who are especially sensitive will notice, along with your physical improvement, a feeling of greater calmness and inner peace. In our wholistic approach, better body functions go hand in hand with improved mind functions, and vice versa. This is what we call a virtuous circle.

During the winter there are always many cases of the flu. When a patient with the flu comes to us, it is important to react quickly. The easiest way to make the essential oils penetrate into the organism is through the skin. The patient sits astride a chair with the back of the chair at his/her chest and warm air (not hot!) is blown on his/her upper back. At home you can use a hair dryer (with regulated heat) on a low setting. When the skin has been gently warmed, a few drops of undiluted essential oils are applied on the upper back. The respiratory blend is well suited for this use.

You can apply the respiratory blend to the soles of your feet, in the same way. You can use a hair dryer to blow the warm air on the skin then apply the oils. With some rest, healthy and light food, and the continuation at home of the external applications, flu infections can be overcome with none of the complications you would suffer from allopathic intervention.

The Inter-rib Massage

Here is another way to apply essential oils on the thorax that can help set free respiratory blockages. To locate these blockages do this simple test. With each thumb follow any pathway between two ribs from as far as you can reach on your back around to the place where the ribs join the sternum. In addition to laughing if you are ticklish, you may notice little knots and crystals that you will feel with your thumbs. Each of these represents a kind of blockage on the energy pathways. Those areas are never properly taken care of. Even if you receive regular massages, it is rare that your therapist, who simply wants to make you feel relaxed, thinks of doing this inter-rib massage. But working on these areas helps the breathing function in general and is also wonderful for other organs as well as the many functions linked with several acupuncture meridians crossed during this massage.

Start at the upper part of the back and massage each inter-rib area several times. Towards the top it is not as easy to feel the spaces between the ribs. It becomes much easier as you progress downward, in particular after you have left the level of the scapula. A good session that focuses intensely on the inter rib spaces may last fifteen minutes. If you feel like laughing during the massage, it's OK. It's an excellent sign of letting go of emotions that may have been blocked inside. And you know that blocked, unexpressed emotions have serious consequences, even in the physical body. The internal organs that are stimulated most by this massage are the liver, spleen, kidneys, adrenal glands, and large intestine. I recommend this massage for everyone, but especially for smokers who are trying to quit and detoxify their bodies, and children or adults with asthma.

Internal use of the respiratory blend

We speak of dosages that range from a trace to a drop. This may seem very small, but keep in mind that this drop represents the equivalent of several handfuls of fresh plants. Use it internally the way you use all the other ingestable oils. An easy way to prepare a purifying and refreshing drink is to insert a toothpick into the vial of essential oil and then stir the toothpick into a glass of pure water. Most oils contribute a wonderful aromatic flavor to the water. It is important to understand that even this trace of the respiratory blend or other essential oils represents a lot of energy. When a trace of oil is diluted in water, the molecules ionize. Ionization means that electrical charges appear at the surface of the molecules. In the respiratory blend there is a good balance of some molecules that are negatively charged and others that are charged positively.

In order to get the greatest benefit from this aromatic water, do not drink it with a meal or snack. Keep it in your mouth for a little while before swallowing it so some of the energy will be absorbed there. As you swallow it on an empty stomach, the absorption will take place very easily and quickly. Millions upon millions of ionized aromatic molecules will circulate in your blood vessels and perform their purification throughout your body. Doing this with warm water makes a quick 'herbal aromatic tea' that is excellent during the cold season.

What people usually call respiration is referred to as "ventilation" by physiologists. Ventilation means air goes in and out, leaving the oxygen to penetrate into the blood and the carbon dioxide to be removed. But in physiology what we call respiration takes place inside the cells, and more precisely inside the mitochondria or the power plants of your cells. It is here that the combustion takes place and energy is released. The respiratory blend has both a ventilation function and a cellular respiratory function on a much deeper level. You will remember that essential oils can cross the cellular membranes carrying their influence very far and very deep. They help your cells burn better creating more energy to think and express creative ideas as well as to move. If you were able to create a synthetic pharmaceutical molecule with such miraculous power, you would surely win the Nobel Prize for medicine! Nature guards most of its most complex secrets when it comes to healthy living, and man searches in vain to duplicate her creations.

Let's now turn our attention to the defense blend.

Chapter 15: The Defense Blend

A newborn comes in contact with a world filled of danger. This is why the very first secretion from its mother's breast glands, known as colostrum, is not primarily a nourishing substance, but rather a strongly protective substance. Nature insists that natural defensive molecules from colostrum must come first. Apart from the obvious physical risks of cold and trauma, the child must face hidden risks until his own built in protective system matures.

Importance of the Immune System

The Latin origin of the word immune comes from the prefix 'im,' meaning negative and 'mune,' meaning money. It literally means with no money. In ancient Rome, those who were immune did not have to pay the Emperor. To be immune to a disease means you do not have to pay the price of having this disease.

The actual discovery of the immune system took place at the turn of the century, about fifty years after the discovery of the microorganisms associated with infectious diseases. That was, as always, only the beginning. And the more we learn today about antigens, B lymphocytes, immunoglobulins G and M, T4 cells, leukocytes, macrophages, and all the other complexities of the immune system, the more there is to learn. There is a fantastic complexity and organization in the immune system. Everything is logical inside the body.

What's more, the immune system is tightly connected to the mind. In fact, I like to describe it as the psycho-neuro-immune system. Negative thoughts and emotions can trigger crazy reactions like autoimmune diseases.

Conversely, positive thoughts and emotions play a major role in restoring it and keeping it in good health. Norman Cousins, in his book, *Anatomy of a Disease,* described how watching hilarious video tapes all day helped him cure his disabling autoimmune condition for which modern medicine had no satisfying answer.

Since essential oils work on both the mind and the body, you can see why they would be powerful assets in supporting the immune system. In fact, I like to call essential oils my 'immune system without' that helps my immune system within.

Let me help you understand the wholistic way in which essential oils work, and the difference between them and antibiotics.

Essential Oils Are the Universal Answer to Infections
Some extreme naturopathic circles insist that there is no such thing as infections. Others minimize their importance. It is as wrong and restrictive to take this position, as it is to view microbes as the sole cause of infectious diseases. The truth is in the middle. There are cases where any delay in cleansing a wound will bring serious consequences, like a rusty nail that pierces your shoe and penetrates deep into the sole of your foot! I have had this dramatic and extremely painful experience twice in my life. And I explained in my previous book how to handle it wholistically and aromatically.

Last week in the news we heard of a man whose foot was pierced by a rusty nail. He immediately went to his general practitioner, who promptly prescribed antibiotics. After a week the foot was worse, and he went back to his doctor who referred his patient to the nearest hospital for a surgical procedure. Unfortunately he only received more antibiotics and some superficial care. A nurse came frequently to his home to help dress the wound.

A week later, the condition had turned so bad that he was rushed to a major hospital. The infection had become generalized and he collapsed in the emergency ward. They discovered that he had developed gangrene and, had he not been rushed to the major hospital, he would have died within the next four hours. The only way to save him was to amputate his leg. When he awoke and discovered that a trifling nail accident, medically mishandled, had lead him to the amputation of his leg, he was in a terrible shock. The financial compensation he received from the first hospital will never give him back his leg or his previous active life.

When I heard this sad story, it made me want to redouble my efforts to get the word out about essential oils. The description that is given in my book, *Natural Home Health Care Using Essential Oils*, would enable you to at least take a few logical first aid steps. Modern doctors have acquired a kind of automatic antibiotic response, and they seem to forget the common sense, basic hygiene procedures and actions that need to be performed, especially in the case of external penetration by a highly infectious nail

Having presented this tragic example, I want to now focus on the aromatic molecules that represent the best answer for bacterial infections.

In French we say, "Cest infect", or "Cest une infection!" when something is revolting or smells bad. This is because the bacteria that normally decompose decaying food multiply and secrete substances which, fortunately in a way, offend our sense of smell and thus warn us about potentially poison food.

At home we try in every way to identify foul odors and get rid of them because deep in our mind they signal danger. If nature clearly sends us such warning signals, it is true that it also provides us with very clear positive signs or 'olfactive signatures.'

The pleasing fragrances that come from aromatic plants tell our brain that they are able to counteract the source of foul odors. We say, "the nose knows," instinctively or intuitively, that the foul smell means disease and death and the aromatic fragrance means the opposite—health and life.

Among the tens of thousands of aromatic molecules, some have a greater ability to attack microorganisms. Let's take a comparative example. A very common way of disinfecting an external wound is the use of alcohol. Alcohol is a general name. The specific name of the molecule is ethanol. Ethanol comes from the fermentation of sugar. Your body knows that alcohol on a wound is painful!

Aromatic plants can manufacture alcohols that are not as aggressive as ethanol. The best example is our well-known and beloved tea tree oil. The leaves of the Melaleuca alternifolia are genetically endowed with a molecule called terpineol-4, which represents up to 40% of its aromatic secretion. If you have ever applied undiluted tea tree oil on a wound, you know that it doesn't trigger as strong a burning sensation as most types of alcohol. The absence of a burning sensation does not mean that it does not "kill the bugs." On the contrary, tea tree oil is our first choice for an anti-infectious substance.

So, we find in aromatic plants such molecules belonging to the category called alcohols, or more precisely monoterpenols.

There is a category of molecules, which has an even greater capacity to "kill disease bugs." They are the phenols. Their stronger scent tells us that their power over pathogenic microorganisms is even stronger.

The Synergy of Alcohols and Phenols

Whenever I teach basic chemistry I bring out my switchblade and show my class the point of the blade to illustrate the anti-infectious power of the phenols! If a very serious danger threatens your life such as a wild animal attack, would you defend your life with the side of the blade, however sharp it is, or would you use the point?

In everyday infections, you use the side of the blade (alcohols) to cut whatever needs to be cut. You use the point (phenols) for only a very limited kind of action (to pierce or to stab). There are very few phenols but many alcohols, with a much greater variety of properties and actions inside the body.

What is even more relevant, the number of aromatic plants that contain phenols is very limited, whereas the number of plants rich in alcohols is very large.

A phenol-rich essential oil must not be applied undiluted on the skin, let alone on an open wound! Even diluted in carrier oil, you have to be very prudent with it. It is like having a potential fire in your hands. You can easily understand that in a first aid kit, I refuse, for safety reasons, to include any phenol-rich essential oils.

Two well-known phenols are thymol and carvacrol, chemically very closely related. They are found in thyme and oregano essential oils. Another phenol is called eugenol, found in clove bud oil. Another molecule that is as strong as the phenols is cinnamic aldehyde that comes from the cinnamon bark of Ceylon or cinnamon twigs from China or Viet-Nam.

Phenols, used in large and regular amounts, create a burden on the liver. Of course, in very serious and acute infections, French medical doctors who work with essential oils are allowed to use them, with relevant precautions. In long-term use, they can be used in blends if they represent a very small amount of the total blend.

Alcohols are the most important oils for our long-term health and vitality. They work in a much more versatile way, not only on many organs, but also on the immune system, in a way that is balanced and harmonious and gentle. Keep in mind that overstimulation is not good.

The best oils for a long-term program of overall health are a combination rich in complementary alcohols, activated by a small amount of essential oils rich in phenols. This has been for me the most efficient general formula, from a disease prevention perspective.

The Molecular Rationale Behind the Defense Blend

When a French medical doctor creates a blend, he looks first at the biochemical groups or functional families to which these molecules belong. In the English style way, which is much more wholistically oriented, the aromatherapist says, "This essential oil is good for this, that essential oil is good for that, etc." The English way works quite well for a general rebalancing.

When it comes to facing a specific or serious medical case, it is better to analyze the situation in a logical manner, finding the different physio-pathological processes that are involved and matching them with the aromatic molecule families that work best. Once the families are identified, we choose more specifically the molecules we want. Once the molecules are selected, we eventually arrive where the English aromatherapist begins—the choice of the individual essential oils.

This approach is used by most of those who received Pierre Franchomme's teaching. *I do not say that it is the only way or even the best one in all cases!* What I do know is that, from a *statistical point of view,* the odds of getting good results from this French approach are fairly good ones.

In creating my defense blend, however I was not trying to help one person with a specific condition, but rather *a very large group of potential users in a very broad way.* I therefore decided to rely first on a combination of different alcohols that complement one another. It was also extremely important that the formula remain affordable using the highest quality of oils (which are the only ones that really work).

My goal to "embrace health" meant that I wished to enhance the immune system of the body by recommending a blend that could be used on a day-to-day basis as well as on a long-term basis. Combining different essential oils that contain molecules from the same biochemical family creates, as you will recall, a horizontal synergy. Here, I have created a horizontal synergy based on six different kinds of alcohol molecules.

The first alcohol that should come to mind is terpineol-4, with its almost universal power. A second alcohol which works quite well with terpineol-4 is geraniol, important in particular for internal purification. The third alcohol that is indispensable is menthol, the super activator of all the defenses of the organism.

With just this first group of three alcohols, we already have a powerful anti-infectious blend. But because we want to go further on this pathway, we will add three more alcohol molecules.

The fourth molecule is linalol. It is powerfully anti-infectious and yet very gentle—one of Natures great secrets that we cannot duplicate. When you add the fact that this essential oil has a spellbinding scent, you have an amazing all-around essential oil.

The fifth monoterpenolic molecule is closely related to the second one: it is called citronnelol. It represents in a way the yang energy side opposite the yin energy of the geraniol.

The sixth monoterpenol is very interesting in the perspective of a balancing action upon the immune system, keeping it under control, precluding it from going too far in its reactions, which sometimes makes it the enemy of its sister cells in the organism (autoimmune disease). This alcohol is borneol.

You can think of this horizontal synergy with six aromatic molecules as being represented by a six-point star, with a molecule at each point. Now, we have to add a plus to this fundamental synergy of monoterpenols. This will be provided by some phenols and cinnamic aldehyde.

It is possible to use the monoterpenols synergy on its own. It is very rich, complex and very whole. But the phenols, at a rate of less than 10% of the total blend, will bring a touch of intensity that is very noticeable. The blend would be incomplete without them. This 'touch' is small enough that the whole blend is quite safe to use. Yet, you can think of the phenols as a way to sharpen action of the blend and endow it with a quick-start effect

.

Lets see now how this molecular logical approach can be transformed into a logical corresponding choice of essential oils.

The Botanical Selection for the Defense Blend

Knowing now the molecules we need to create this synergy, we look for the essential oils that contain them. In doing so, we still know that, since we are using natural oils, there are many other molecules in each oil, other than the primary one we are seeking. And they have many more actions than just the main one of the prevailing molecule.

We test essential oils through gas chromatography to determine that they do, in fact, have the anticipated measure of the desired molecule. Each batch of essential oil must be tested in this way to be sure the formula will do what it is supposed to do.

When we examine the gas chromatograms of various high quality essential oils, we find the following match-up with key constituents and essential oils:

terpineol-4 is found in **tea tree**
geraniol is found in **palmarosa**
menthol is found in **peppermint**
linalol is found in **Michelia alba** (leaves)
citronnelol is found in **geranium** from China
borneol is found in **Moroccan thyme**

For some molecules, the botanical choice is obvious or very simple, like for instance for tea tree for terpineol-4, or peppermint for menthol or Moroccan Thyme (Thymus satureioides) for borneol.

For linalol, it is not as obvious. Rosewood, Ho leaves and *Michelia alba* leaves all offer high rates of linalol. Rosewood essential oil raises ecological concerns, so we leave it out. Because *Michelia alba* belongs to the *Magnioliaceae* family, the one that began the flower revolution on planet earth, just after the Conifers, it has my preference.

Concerning geranium, although the Egyptian variety is in the singles kit, here it is the Chinese one that is required, because of its much higher content in citronnelol.

This blend offers both a nice scent and a powerful activity against infectious agents. Because of the Moroccon thyme, we also have a certain amount of a phenol called carvacrol. To increase the phenols, some eugenol- and thymol-rich essential oils are added, in a small proportion (less than 10% of the total).

Those used to the usual non-molecular approach to blending are surprised when they experience the defense blend for the first time. They always acknowledge that there is something deeply special about it, compared to other aromatherapy blends they are familiar with. It is a rich symphony, a harmonious concentrate of matter, energy and information, endowed with a purifying and revitalizing potential that goes far beyond the power of a single essential oil.

Understanding the Overall Power of the Defense Blend

Superficially if we were looking for the equivalent of the defense blend among the single essential oils, we would think of tea tree. But we have reached a much higher dimension with this carefully designed blend. I created in this blend an essential oil mixture that no single essential oil can match. Still, I would be disappointed if using the defense blend kept anyone from using tea tree oil by itself. It would be like saying, "now that I have a symphony, I no longer enjoy the song of the birds."

Let us now discuss the world of bacteria and fungi that live inside us—more specifically, inside our intestines. As a medical doctor I have prescribed a lot of essential oils for ingestion. They can play an immense role, not only in clearing the body, but also the mind. I am not suggesting that a person who is fundamentally wicked or perverted will change overnight by using essential oils! I honestly think that the realm of spiritual evolution has its own principles and rules.

But I can remember so many of my patients who were completely destroyed, mentally, emotionally, and psychologically by of years of taking antibiotics, plus an array of psychoactive drugs. They had their life renewed when they found the aromatic way.

One big difference between classical English aromatherapy and the French aromatic way is that normally the English way excludes ingestion. I can perfectly understand and respect their position, *particularly when you so often see inferior essential oils that are potentially harmful because of poor distillation, adulteration or solvent extraction.* Here is a simple anecdote to make you aware of the benefit in going beyond simple external use.

Marie Céline, a lady in her forties, began to use essential oils for the prevention of a repeated sore throat, especially during the cold and flu season. She had heard about essential oils from her father who had used essential oils for the same problem. (I had prescribed two blends for her father—one for external application and one for internal use.) She did a topical application on the lymph nodes on the sides of her neck, using the external blend I had made for her father. However, she did nothing with the internal blend I had recommend be used on the tongue at the onset of infection.

Whereas the lymphatic external application is highly recommended procedure, its role is only a complementary one. Marie-Céline got through the early part of the flue season, but later on had a bout of tonsillitis. The external diluted application on the lymphatic nodes had played its role, but it had reached its limit short of what was required.

The disease came on after the holidays, as is often the case, since the real origin of a sore throat comes from the inside of the body and not from a microbe who jumps down her throat! She went back to the antibiotics her doctor prescribed to her. As usual, they seemed to work at first but the sore throat started up again with greater force three weeks later!

This time she took antibiotics plus some cortisone! It was the "beating up stage" which, once more, merely concealed the symptoms and pushed the toxins a little deeper inside. A month later, the tonsillitis was there again. This time her father told her to try applying my internal blend on her tongue and swallowing the aromatic saliva. It worked very well and very quickly, to her great surprise. At this point Marie-Céline decided to undergo a real aromatic treatment. Under my guidance, she began regular ingestion of essential oils, in order to reach the source of the problem inside the digestive system itself, and this, with some nutritional correction solved her problem in depth. She learned that, as soon as any sign of a sore throat appeared, she should immediately apply the blend on her tongue. And she carried the blend with her from then on.

The day is not far off when a grand unification will take place, and the external English approach will unite with the French internal approach.

As you study with me, we will go ever deeper into the influence of the bacterial and fungal world involved in all diseases. Their influence is felt or found in all the organs and all the systems, including the psyche, the endocrine system, the nervous system, and, of course, directly and indirectly, on the immune system itself. This first introductory book is not the place to report extremely advanced case histories, but I am sure you can begin to appreciate the potential essential oils have for us in the future.

Let me tell you more about the world of microorganisms and a conflict between the famous Louis Pasteur and another great French scientist and founder of experimental medicine named Claude Bernard. Pasteur had focused his entire work on the role of the microbes, whereas Claude Bernard thought in a more wholistic way, paying his attention on what we call in French "the terrain" or breeding ground of the disease.

It is reported in many naturopathic books that as Pasteur was lying on his bed waiting for death to come, he uttered : " *Cest Claude Bernard qui a raison. Le microbe nest rien; cest le terrain qui est tout.* It is

Claude Bernard who is right. The microbe is nothing; it is the breeding ground of the disease that is everything."

Being more on the naturopathic side than on the official medical one, I am tempted to rejoice on hearing this sentence pronounced by the discoverer of microbes and jump to hasty conclusions. Yet, such a response would be wrong.

Whenever you hear words like 'always, never, all, none, nothing, everything, everybody, nobody,' and the like, especially in the world of biology, they do not correspond to the reality of this world. Because of the hundreds of analyses I have performed on my patients who had infections where the bacteria was isolated, and because of the way this bacteria reacted to essential oils tested in the lab, I have come to an unusual conclusion.

I found sometimes that the same bacteria, lets say a staphylococcus, are sensitive to the specific essential oils that *correspond exactly to the "terrain" of the patient who hosts this bacteria!* One is then forced to admit that, *" Le microbe, cest tout, car le microbe, cest le terrain.* The microbe is everything because the microbe creates its own breeding ground.

Here is a critical point that underscores the importance of regular preventive use of the defense blend. I can't emphasize this enough. **The roots of disease are present long before the disease actually manifests itself. These roots are activated by microorganisms and their toxins, the immune system's reaction to them, and the workings of the mind. As long as this hidden yet impending source of infection is active, no genuine healing can take place.**

The only way to work on, expose and eliminate deeply concealed infections is to turn to essential oils. One of the main reasons infections are hidden so deep inside us is because of the shameful way mankind has played with antibiotics, not only on the doctors side, but even worse on the veterinary and animal breeding side, purely for the sake of making quick dollars. Antibiotics help animals put on weight more quickly so they can be sent to the slaughterhouse sooner and increase profit magins. As a concerned medical doctor who has studied them, antibiotics are the last answer I would ever use in treating disease. After half a century of completely devious and crazy overuse of antibiotics, it is time for mankind to return to the source of life through the gift of aromatic plants. America is now ready to receive the message of freedom that, at least on the medical side, originated in France.

Bartholdi offered to the United States the Statue of Liberty. We are now ready to open the gateway leading to freedom from the pressures of the pharmaceutical lobbies and the destruction of antibiotic overuse. If we all begin to earnestly learn about and use essential oils, integrated into a whole approach of natural health, *the role of synthetic drugs will be reduced to specific emergencies or extremely advanced diseases.* For the largest part of the population, natural hygiene accompanied by plants and essential oils will keep them *healthy and vital from birth to a very old age.* This makes the role of our defense blend a crucial one.

The External Daily Use of the Defense Blend

The way we use this blend is no surprise. There is a way to use the defense blend for acute conditions, for chronic problem, and for preventative care. There is also a way of taking advantage of its power for what I call "evolution enhancing care."

The blend is designed for both internal and external use. Of course, the external use quickly reaches its limit because the first and foremost hidden part of all infection is inside the bowel.

Pouring out a 10 ml vial of the blend and massaging it on the outside of the abdomen is less effective (and more costly) than ingesting a few drops in honey with water or applying a few traces on the tongue.

I want you to understand the importance of accompanying the external application of the blend with a special mental attitude. This small idea is going to make a very big difference to you in the end. Please understand that we are in a program in which a long-term habit is implemented, and not an intense struggle to fight an acute infection. We are embracing total health, not fighting a quick symptom of a disease.

We know that the defense blend contains a certain small amount of strong molecules like phenols. Though it is not a large percentage of the formula, the presence of these powerful molecules signals us to be careful of possible allergic reactions. The area, as you know, that is always easy and safe to use is the sole of each foot. We know that essential oil can be applied neat there. In any case, the penetration is fairly swift. It is an easy way to bring billions of powerful 'living molecules' into your body. Here is how I would describe it.

Just as you would savor the flavor of a first bite of a peach after fasting for a long time, you want to take the vial containing the defense blend in your left hand and enjoy the pleasure of the aroma in a state of receptivity and openness. If you do this you will begin to feel the immense concentrated power of this precious liquid. In this 10 ml you have the equivalent of a huge amount of plant material that has been brought together from all over the world. Use the healing power of gratitude for these plants and all those who have worked together growing, distilling, shipping, blending, and teaching you about them. Do not neglect to thank the Creator of all this marvelous complexity in the plant kingdom as well as your body and mind. Enjoy the spirit of this blend as you would a garden of wild flowers. Hold the vial at a distance from your nose and let the aroma come to you in a subtle yet real way. As you take time for this gentler, less brutal approach, you will feel a greater psycho-neuro-endocrine-immune response that represents a crucial part of your whole healing program.

This minute, spent doing nothing but breathing and smelling will become a treat for your mind and body, which you will look forward to more and more. To bypass this initial step would be to invade your inner space prematurely. The ancients thought of their body as a temple and the offerings were considered sacred. Use this time to create in your mind a full awareness of the enormous results you can receive from this complex blend.

Place your left foot on your right knee. Again, the gesture should not be a purely mechanical one. A first drop is applied on the anterior or ball of the foot; a second drop is applied on the center, and the third drop is applied on the posterior or heel. Here, the purpose is not a massage as in foot reflex therapy, but rather an almost immediate absorption of the oils.

Turn the tips of your fingers very gently three times clockwise on each drop, and it's done. Do the same thing on the right foot, placed on your

left knee. It takes you two minutes to do the whole thing, and what a powerful benefit you receive from this wholistic treatment!
Adapt the procedure to your personal reactions and perceptions. If a drop is too much for you, use a trace. I have no intention of pushing you into using a large quantity of the oil. The regularity is for me far more important. And you will find that a deep transformation will take place inside your body and mind, and both known and hidden infections will progressively taper off and disappear.

Morning appears to be the best time for using this blend. However, this blend has *an overall balancing action*. Even an evening application, if it is better for you, does not appear to disturb sleep patterns. Experiment for yourself.

As I stated before, the power of the defense blend goes far beyond the elimination of microbes. This blend has the capacity, for those who are receptive, to induce a profound action of clarification, pacification, and strengthening of the mind. And this deep action on the psyche also helps the immune system perform its task harmoniously and efficiently.

I would even go as far as to say that the way you train or reeducate your immune cells to function properly is similar to the way you receive training in martial arts. You no longer think of your immune cells as being aggressive as in a war! You visualize your lymphocytes and your leukocytes as being powerful cells capable of bringing down any opponent with calmness and ease, being strongly supported in their task by the aromatic influence that they receive from the regular use of essential oils. All these mental exercises are part of your new aromatic way of life.

You will then wish to dilute the oil in a carrier oil before you apply it to a few more areas of the body. If you intend to give aromatic care to yourself using the defense blend daily for a week or longer, you can prepare diluted aromatic oil for several days' use. But it is always better to blend the oils fresh each day.

Mix five to eight drops of the defense blend in 10 ml of carrier oil. The concentration could be higher when you wish to treat more acute conditions, but here we are focusing on long term use, aside from any specific manifested disease.

Massage this diluted blend for thirty seconds in the area of the spleen, the liver, the kidneys, and the thymus (under the sternum). To assist the lymphatic areas, apply a small amount on the upper groin (do not come too close to the genital area), on the thoracic part of the armpit (not deep inside it) and on the sides of the neck. With this you are surrounded by a kind of protective aromatic aura. Your immune system is prepared to enter the external world, with a clear mind and open heart. Your body is fit, calm, strong, and peaceful. This external shield is harmoniously complemented by the internal intake.

Using the Defense Blend Internally

When I teach those trained in English style aromatherapy about the internal use of essential oils, I explain, that 'olfaction is the way of the young prince and the young princess, external application is the way of the older prince and princess, ingestion is the way of the king and the queen!' Each aspect is important

You may try to obtain results just by smelling for an hour or a whole day and you would not get the same result as ingestion because you need to purify the intestinal flora. An excessive external application on the abdomen is simply a waste of the precious product. One type of use cannot replace the others. Each is unique in its power to work on the body/mind, and each has also its limitations. The beauty and power of integral aromatherapy comes from the combination of the three ways—nose, skin, and mouth.

You have reached a point in your life when you feel it is time for a big change. You realize that Life, with a capital 'L', is not the life you are now living, filled with stress and health complications. It does not take a trip to meditate in the Himalayas to make this change. The change is a question of mental attitude supported by our life companions, the aromatic plants, represented by their essence—their essential oils. The time has come for you to begin the purification process. You choose to start this in-depth cleansing with the defense blend.

The first function of the blend is to trigger purification deep inside your digestive system, starting in the mouth itself. And it will pass to the pharynx, along the esophagus, inside the whole stomach, in the duodenum, the jejunum, the ileum and, finally, inside the colon itself.

The best way to accomplish this is to create a lipidic/glucidid aromatic complex. At home, there is an easy way to make this aromatic synergy for the digestive system. In a cup, count twenty drops of a virgin cold pressed organic oil. Add one drop of the defense blend and mix it thoroughly. Then add a teaspoon of natural honey, and again mix it thoroughly. The honey and oil allows the aromatic molecules of the blend to be included with nutritional molecules. This will enable the blend to go all the way through the digestive pathway. Take an amount the size of a pea on your tongue and melt it with your saliva to help purify your ear, nose, and throat.

Pour a cup of lukewarm water slowly over the rest of the blend in the cup, and stir it clockwise. Breathe in the aroma while it mixes with the water. Remember your thoughts of gratitude. Drink the cup by little sips, keeping them in the mouth a little while before swallowing. As you drink, think of acquiring a healthy intestinal flora that constitutes the foundation of radiant health, the cornerstone of a strong and adaptable immune system, the pillar of nervous, endocrine and psychological balance.

Follow this deep purification process for three weeks and you will experience that deep change that leads from a dull life to a vibrant Life on all levels.

Internal Use of the Defense Blend

You can also use the defense blend in more down-to-earth conditions. But whenever you use the blend, always use your imagination to bring thoughts of gratitude and a perception of the work accomplished inside of you. You will be able to taste the geranium, palmarosa, or *Michelia alba*. These are not the most flavorful oils. Some essential oils may be very nice to smell but taste strange in the mouth. Yet these oils are not at all aggressive and will gently and surely eliminate the toxic elements and protect the good ones inside your intestinal flora.

One way to enhance the taste and make it more palatable is to use it with a drop of lemon essence or a trace of peppermint. These two are best suited for masking the taste of any essential oil or blend.

In the case of acute infectious disease, we have other possibilities. The normal French medical way is to swallow gel caps filled with diluted essential oils. They are easy to prepare and their action is very powerful. You can use essential oil in honey for a sore throat, but when the goal is to accomplish a cleansing of the whole digestive system, gel caps may be a simpler route. Vegetable gel caps (without animal gelatin) are now sold in most health food stores. The ones we purchase in France come from the US.

You open the capsule and count about four drops of the chosen essential oil or blend. Fill up the capsule with an organic, cold pressed vegetable oil, and close the capsule. It is ready to be swallowed. You may vary the number of drops from one to six, four drops being the average.

You can prepare the gel caps ahead of time and take them throughout the day, at lunch for example. But do not prepare too many at a time. The essential oils may partially dissolve the gel cap if they are kept for more than a few days.

I advise you to swallow the gel cap in the middle of the meal or snack rather than at the beginning, so that it won't fall on an empty stomach. If you always insist on high quality oils diluted in organic vegetable oil, and if the gel cap is absorbed with the meal, it seems to be perfectly absorbed by the digestive system. This is the easiest and quickest way to manage current infectious conditions. In more serious cases, take a gel cap each hour throughout the day with only soft fruits or vegetable soups, but no 'hard food.' This will allow the body to become totally purified.

Let me report a case where the internal intake of essential oils is absolutely indispensable: travel in a warm, tropical climate where you can barely escape digestive infection.

Pierre and Sophie are a young couple who were planning a trip to Egypt in the summertime. The travel agent warned them about the possibility intestinal trouble while in Egypt. She called this infection *'la tourista'* meaning that this type of diarrhea is very common among foreign visitors. Instead of taking with them allopathic drugs, Pierre and Sophie chose my defense blend.

They took a gel cap of this blend, diluted in carrier oil, three times a day, one at each meal. If symptoms appeared, they increased the dosage to two gel caps with each meal. The results were interesting. They were traveling with a group, and most of the other travelers, who were not under aromatic protection, experienced the predicted intestinal problems. For some it was so serious that it spoiled their vacation.

Pierre and Sophie took their internal aromatic prevention and experienced no symptoms at all. The difference was so striking that a few friends asked for their secret and they helped them.

Another piece of advice I gave them was to take a small spray bottle with a mixture of water and a drop of lemon and peppermint essential oils for cooling. This brought relief from the stifling hotness of the climate.

This story reminds us that being immune is 'not having to pay the price.' Pierre and Sophie had chosen to pay a small price in advance so that they would not be obliged to pay a much higher price while in Egypt.

In a similar context, but with even greater risk of tropical disease, I remember a situation in Madagascar. As you know, the niaouli essential oil used in my blends comes from this island.
I have several friends who regularly visit Madagascar for business and aromatic agricultural projects. Some follow the normal medical protection but others rely entirely on essential oils for their protection against multiple risks.

A good friend of mine named Patrick told us that when he was in Madagascar, he applied essential oils on his body every day and poured in his drinking water a soluble form of essential oils. He accompanied this with a mosquito net around the bed each night. This enabled him to stay free from any disease. Essential oils have the power to work even at a high degree of risk. I must add that Patrick, who is a great fruit lover, does not refrain from eating the fruits of the island that tourists are normally advised to avoid.

Patrick told me that he was dismayed to see that even though the people of Madagascar have all the aromatic plants and their essential oils available, they still use allopathic drugs and antibiotics while they export their aromatic wealth to the western countries. One of Patrick's generous projects is a clinic where they will re-learn to use this aromatic wealth for their own health. Good luck, Patrick

The Role and Purpose of Internal Use of Essential Oils
Lets start with a case of tonsillitis. Nature takes care of us by creating specific defense organs where the body enters in contact with the external world. For the nose, there are adenoid growths that represent a protective barrier for the air we breathe. The role of the tonsils is to protect us from the foods that are swallowed. This means that the real use for the tonsils is at the inside of the digestive system. When the tonsils are infected, the main reason is not that an external aggressor jumped into the throat or came through bacteria hidden in a piece of food that found its place inside the tonsils!

There is indeed a link with the foods that are absorbed. But this link is an indirect one. How does it occur? We already spoke of congestive toxicosis or toxemia. In natural hygiene, this is considered the number one mechanism for any disease. In reality, in natural hygiene, the very conception of disease is totally different. When the level of congestive toxicosis reaches a dangerous threshold in the blood, in the lymph, and in organs like the liver, the vital force of the body decides to undertake its own purification/elimination process. Doctors call this a disease or an illness and are sincerely convinced that they must do all they can to 'fight' the disease which they give a very complicated name so it may sound highly scientific. But disease is merely the alarm signal for the body that says, 'enough is enough.' Disease shows us that the time has come for some type of 'spring cleaning.'

So, we arrive at this paradoxical situation where highly trained professionals do all that they can to suppress something that is intended to purify and eventually to heal your body. After acute diseases have been repressed so repetitively with so many chemical drugs, the body decreases the intensity and the frequency of its efforts. A point comes where the chronic disease settles or even a degenerative condition appears and this becomes an altogether different and potentially life-threatening situation.

In short, with this approach to disease, modern medicine is preparing its future patients, to manifest every conceivable infection and disease. The role of microorganisms has been misunderstood. In the great majority of current infectious diseases *(not necessarily all of them)*, including the widespread ear, nose, throat and bronchial infections, the bacteria that are found in those cavities and in the rejected secretions come in reality *from the inside the organism,* and not from the outside world. The bacteria become 'deviant' or 'delinquent' and then pathogenic, because of the conditions that are created inside the digestive tract.

The bacteria have the capacity to migrate, in the same way as the white blood cells, and to colonize any other parts of the body. If a lot of waste matter leaves the digestive system and arrives in the respiratory system to be expelled, the bacteria will accompany it and begin to thrive actively on it. Incidentally, bacteriologists know that they can enormously accelerate the multiplication of bacteria in test cultures by including in the growth medium—chocolate! Bacteria love chocolate whether outside or inside the body.

French people have huge holiday meals with large amounts of chocolate, and we always face an enormous outbreak of lung and ear, nose, and throat infections approximately twenty days after the end of the feasts. In case of respiratory infections, do you honestly think that simply breathing aromatic particles using aerosols and inhalers will be sufficient to put the infection under control?

Knowing that a huge flow of bacteria migrates from deep inside the body, in the digestive system and in the colon, accompanied by the source of the abnormal glue-like mucous, can you see that there is only one logical solution? We must go to the root and have the aromatic molecules come directly in contact with the digestive system itself.

The other uses of essential oils are only secondary (skin) and tertiary (inhalation) measures that do not have sufficient power to reach the internal source of the infection. You may think of your digestive system as a Trojan horse, with many hidden, potentially dangerous soldiers. As long as they are well fed, according to the laws of natural nutrition, they remain quiet and even prove their usefulness for the entire body. When they receive large amounts of dead industrial foods, the kind that prevails in the fast food industry, they become our enemies. Or should I say that they operate in a logical way that ought to make the ill person become aware of the faults of hygiene in his/her life, and then decide to change the illness producing habits.

Because of my deep conviction that the basis of health lies in sound nutrition before anything else, I cannot imagine teaching the internal use of essential oils in medical schools or pharmaceutical universities, unless the professors and doctors accept the laws of a wholistic approach to health. Can you imagine a patient having received only an anti-infectious aromatic prescription with essential oils in capsules, and getting them from his pharmacist? Neither his doctor nor his chemist will have made the least effort to explain to him the real source of his infection, and the necessity to change his nutritional behavior and his choice of foods. What happens? It' s noon and he rushes to the nearest fast food restaurant. You catch sight of him, swallowing the gel cap containing the most evolved aromatic formulation ever conceived, with the purest essential oils available on earth, accompanied by a Big Mac and a Coke!

I am sure you can see the grotesque and ludicrous character of such a screenplay. No, you can see that no global effort is made for a wholistic approach to true health. I rather see my teaching role with the lay persons who are open and willing to change their lives, than with the 'big guys' who practice medicine like 'automatic drug-prescribing machines' without taking any time to educate their patients in how to become the authors of their own health.

The struggle of all my life is an integrated form of practicing medicine, but with whole foods and natural medicine at the summit of the teaching and at the core of the practice.

Confirmation Through Both Research and Practice

I received my initiation in scientific aromatherapy through Pierre Franchomme. We parted ways when the book we co-authored, *L' aromathérapie exactement,* was published in 1990. His way led him eventually to become director of a research laboratory in phytoaromatherapy (in Bucharest, Rumania). There, he has the required budget and the sophisticated equipment to perform advanced research, to prove experimentally

the worth of essential oils. A major field of his research deals precisely with infection and the inflammatory and immune response of the body to it.
The latest summary of this research was presented in March 1998 in Grasse, France during the First Symposium on Integrated Aromatic Medicine and Scientific Aromatherapy (the proceedings are available through Essential Science Publishing in an English translation). It dealt precisely with understanding the role of the intestinal flora, both in the occurrence of diseases of all kinds, and in restoring a state of good health through a proper health management system including nutrition and internal intake of essential oils.

A specific aspect of the research program was to measure the activity of a category of immune cells called neutrophilic leukocytes (you know them as white cells in the blood). Those who wish can read the full text, but I want to simply highlight the fact that the neutrophils, in their efforts to counteract pathogenic micro-organisms, manufacture a lot of substances that, even if they are necessary for the counter-offensive or the attack, prove to be, in a way, deleterious. In particular, they manufacture and secrete free radicals in large amounts, and those free radicals in their turn become a major source of inflammation.

Pierre Franchomme's research confirmed the necessity of continuing the internal use of essential oils over a sufficient period. Starting an internal purification program just to forsake it after a few days is really not beneficial! Your body just starts to feel some relief from the aromatic internal work (even if it is not yet felt consciously), and suddenly it is deprived of its 'aromatic light' and falls back into its night of disease. Please, don't do that to your body.

Two or three weeks of continuous treatment is a good start. In very serious cases you will feel the difference if you stop your internal intake! Your body that was ill for decades and bombarded with heaps of chemical drugs can only be restored to health using a whole year's program.

For ladies who have menstrual cycles, we often prescribe three weeks of internal intake in a row. Then they stop for five to seven days during menstruation and resume for three more weeks. This can be done over several months in chronic cases. I think in particular of systemic candidiasis where aromatherapy can prove lifesaving for those women who were brought to this dreadful situation because of antibiotic abuse! In future writings I will report striking case histories of recoveries from chronic candidiasis. For those ladies, essential oils are seen as genuine lifesavers.

My purpose is not to push anyone plagued with such a condition into strong treatments on his/her own, but rather to encourage you to undertake a complete program with trained natural health professionals where integral aromatherapy will play a major role along with the other natural treatments. The purpose of this book is to pass around information, not to replace the work of so many excellent natural-health-oriented professionals who work in the United States and Canada.

With the growing collaboration with aromatically oriented French doctors, we will succeed in building a strong North American/French connection in the same way that a strong link was built with the United Kingdom in opening the English style aromatherapy to the medical side.

Conclusion

By studying the defense blend you have come to a clearer understanding of the way I create a strong synergistic blend. You are better able to understand the nature of psychological experiences that can come from using this purification blend. You also know how to use your blend daily in a convenient way, and what to do to become more and more independent in the management of your health.

You know how to use your blend externally for activating the immune system, and you can understand the necessity of going to the root of the bacterial invasion by ingesting the oils in a way that is both safe and efficient.

You see the necessity of following long term programs, especially when years and decades of wrong living, toxic nutrition, and absorption of chemical drugs have almost completely ruined the body's initial potential for health and vitality.

The defense blend represents a major step, probably the most important one, in your aromatic initiation. The respiratory blend and the defense blend represent the two main aromatic pillars in the reconstruction and rebuilding of your health and vitality. The third pillar has another major complementary role to play, and it deserves all our attention. Lets find out what interesting surprises it has for us.

Chapter 16: The Exercise Blend

To be alive is to move. It is also to reach, to stretch, to lift, and to turn.

The study of this third blend will help you use the wonderful aromatic molecules of essential oils to achieve your full range of movement for a healthy and vital life.

A Fundamental Triangle of Health

To run properly, a car must have the a) right machinery, b) the right additives (oil and gasoline), and c) a driver. Without all three, the car won't get very far. If the car stays in the garage all year long and the driver only drives once a year, even the best machinery won't work very well.

Regular activity is one of the sources of life and good health, for the body as well as for the mind. It is *by moving your limbs that your lungs and heart are activated and function properly.* Movement is a simple way to create harmony within the body and the mind. Just imagine what we would be without it.

Think of an overweight teenager who never exercises. She binges as she watches TV, rarely if ever exercises, and refuses to go out with friends. This is a typical vicious cycle made more serious by low self-esteem. The more depressed she feels, the more she compensates by bingeing on unhealthy foods. The greater the weight gain, the less comfortable she feels among her friends and the less she feels like exercising.

We all know that preaching to a depressed teenager doesn't work. It only increases the depression. Forbidding food or TV or other privileges doesn't work for long. Forcing her to go to parties and meetings with other young people is a waste of time. But starting a program of modest physical exercise can often solve in a very happy way what may have appeared to be totally impossible at first glance. There is a kind of magic in physical exercise that suddenly makes simple, things that once appeared very difficult to change.

Exercise begins a change in the mental attitude as well. Attitudes toward food change. Bingeing stops, and it becomes easier to choose healthy foods. Weight begins to come off, friends come around more often, and a healthier cycle is restored.

Movement is vital for recovering both physical and psychological health. I personally feel that among the greatest benefactors of mankind are the inventors of the running shoe.

Like the car, there are three essential ingredients in good health—nutrition, positive thinking, and exercise. Exercise is usually the easiest to implement. And it usually jump-starts the other two. Physical movement costs you very little. It is a brisk walk, a simple jog, an invigorating swim, or some refreshing aerobics. It is available in one form or another to anyone.

Exercise increases oxygen in the lungs, helps blood circulation throughout the body, and helps the lungs eliminate toxins. It helps all the organs function better. Without exercise organs lose some of their ability to function well. Exercise also creates positive changes in mental areas of life including the will to achieve and the power to master self. It begins a virtuous cycle of positive change.

It is most important to begin gently and progress gradually. Don't compete with anyone but yourself, always listening to and respecting the messages your body sends you.

Some Anatomical Basics of Exercise

As I am writing this chapter, I am learning to walk again after an aggravated and inflamed sprain to my left ankle. Crutches were my companions for three weeks. I have learned first hand that applying neat essential oils on an inflamed area does not work because it only adds to the fire and the pain. I felt it in every joint of my left foot and ankle! Even diluting the oils with carrier oil did not bring relief. I was only able to draw the fire out of my foot and ankle with cold floral water compresses and cold clay poultices.

Remember the difference between a simple bone fracture and a serious sprain. Once a broken bone is repaired and healed, it usually becomes even stronger at the place of the fracture. But in the case of a serious sprain, the elongated and torn ligaments may remain quite sensitive and be made even more fragile, especially in the case of repeated sprains.

When considering the question of movement, our attention has to focus first of all on the mobile parts, i.e. on the joints, and secondarily on the muscles and on the nerves that enable their contraction. Then comes the condition of the heart and the lungs and of course the psychological aspect which plays a more important role than many realize.

We live in a civilization that tends to make us lazy! It is obvious that our great grand parents moved a great deal more than we do. In our day, if we do not steadfastly schedule some kind of regular physical exercise, our body becomes rusty, especially the joints. And our muscles lose strength and suppleness. Our minds and willpower become weak as well.

Respecting Your Joints

The study of anatomy in western societies teaches that a joint is merely the way for two bone ends to connect with each other and move. This Western approach is accurate as far as it goes. But if you study and practice yoga, or Chinese energetic exercises, you learn that within your body/mind unit, especially within the joints, are many more hidden aspects of the wonderful human structure! There is a lot they don't yet teach you at the Harvard School of Medicine.

Earlier we learned as we talked about the respiratory system, that the health of our entire body depends, first of all, on good nutrition. This is also abundantly true of healthy joints.

There are two things to avoid in your diet if you want to protect your joints. The first is sugar. Commercially refined sugars (white sugar, corn syrup, etc) are not whole, living foods at all. In their concentrated forms they are particularly harmful to your joints. And remember that there are hundreds of hidden ways sugar gets into your body—dry cereals, soda, fruit drinks, ketchup, desserts—the list is endless!

The other category to restrict is excessive proteins, particularly red meat. Too much acidity—especially if you do not live in a climate where citrus fruits are grown and if you have a nervous temperament—

will prove harmful to your health generally and to your joints in particular. If you are prone to uric acid deposits (which are at the origin of gout and other hidden forms of pains in the joints, muscles, tendons, and nerves), beware of the following categories of foods:

- Chocolate is definitely out!
- Coffee and tea have to be controlled. There are many ways to substitute healthy herbal teas, especially the ones you learned to make using essential oils and natural honey.
- Caviar and other fish eggs containing high amounts of purins should be avoided. But even an excess of soybeans or soy products may be detrimental because they contain purins that raise your uric acid.

When toxins have accumulated in the body and in the joints, a healthy diet should be accompanied by hydrotherapy to help accelerate the elimination of poisons. Warm aromatic salt baths will help this elimination, especially if they are ended with a quick cold shower.

For the sake of your lungs and heart, never start an exercise program without correcting your diet. Always think and act wholistically in this way.

For your psychological health, choose exercise activities that you like. If you have to force yourself to exercise, it won't do as much good, and your exercise program probably won't last very long either!

If you are an exercise novice, it is important to get a check up from a specialist like a chiropractor or an osteopath. If you have been a smoker or have had an unhealthy diet, a second check up with your cardiologist is strongly recommended.

Once all those prerequisites are met, you can begin a wonderfully energizing exercise program complementing it with my wonderful Exercise blend.

How I Created the Blend for Exercise

First of all, I am very grateful for the broad selection of essential oils that are available to us in this day and age. We who live in Western countries have access to hundreds of essential oils from all over the world. But much of the world's population cannot afford to import them, and must rely on a limited number of locally produced essential oils, sometimes only one or two. Should we feel sorry for them? The truth is that they use their local essential oils for almost anything and everything. And guess what? They bring quite good results!

So, you can appreciate that the few single oils I recommend for your beginning essential oil kit offer an enormous wealth of opportunities. And with the blends, it becomes a fortune.

A doctor or pharmacist trained in Western medicine is used to using a highly specific molecule made for a single task inside the organism. With this orientation, the multi-purpose abilities of essential oils are hard to fully appreciate and comprehend. Yet in southern France, it is well known that lavender essential oil is good for many different problems. In Sicily, lemon oil is used for almost everything, too. If you go to New Caledonia, the essential oil of niaouli is used for dozens of conditions. It is used as much for respiratory conditions as it is for treating wounds, burns, and rheumatism. When I am asked how a single essential oil can have such a wide array of applications, I answer, "It's simply life helping life."

A narrow-minded scientist might feel this answer makes him no wiser. And that is sad. An open-minded scientist will recognize that the way nature works is fundamentally wholistic and highly complex. And he will be willing to shift his paradigm. I can accompany him on this mental journey, using the language of science. But we must travel within the framework of what is called 'the science of complexity' (or general system theory) and it is a long and arduous road.

There is a simpler approach and that is to trust nature. As my friend Don Tolman says, "Nature is very complicated, so we don't have to be."

Let's return now to the exercise blend and review its multiple potentials. We might be tempted to call it the blend for activating and warming joints and muscles. And there is nothing wrong in saying that. But the power of this blend goes further than that. It has the power to activate many functions in the body as well as the mind and emotions. Whenever I do what I call the "all joints" application with my exercise blend (covered later in this chapter) the very first thing I feel is an increase in energy. And second, I feel my entire respiratory system being opened and activated. Naturally, my joints also benefit deeply from the regular use of the Exercise blend.

> I remember the case of a male patient in his forties who consulted me for a serious respiratory condition. His doctor diagnosed the condition as a form of tuberculosis (although it turned out to be linked to an autoimmune process). I gave this patient and his wife a complete program using essential oils to be followed every day. He ingested diluted oils orally and also took some by rectal injections. He also used aromatic aerosols and external applications of neat essential oils. He followed my instructions meticulously for an entire year with consultations every month or two. There was, of course, a stabilization and later a real improvement in the condition of his lungs. But more interestingly, the patient told me he had previously been bothered by pains in several joints and in his spine. We had not focused attention on these because they were not his main concern. But at the end of the year, he acknowledged that, in addition to feeling much better on the respiratory side, the joint and spinal pains had vanished. This is an excellent example of what any serious and steady aromatic program can bring about throughout the body.

A daily massage with the exercise blend can help loosen stiff joints. Or, if you are already supple and fit, the massage will prepare you mentally and physically for exercise and movement. But the blend will do much more for you than that.

The aim of the exercise blend is not to stop pain, as you would do by applying peppermint. Its first purpose is to bring the stimulating energy of aromatic plants into your whole organism. Especially in the joints, essential oils can accelerate circulation and release blockage. essential oils do not work in the same way as "quick fix," medical methods. The deterioration and degeneration of joints is a process that takes place over years of accumulated nutritional faults combined with poor exercise or unbalanced and excessive exercise for some joints. Recovery requires time, and a complete program, in which the exercise blend plays a vital role.

Use the Exercise Blend as a Warming Blend Only

Here is another crucial point. Roughly speaking, a painful joint may be inflamed or "hot," or it may be in a stiff, blocked, "cold energy" state. The exercise blend is intended to bring a *warming energy.* It is not recommended for inflamed muscles or joints, especially in the acute state.

The exercise blend is energizing. Don't apply it before going to bed unless you want to be alert for some kind of nighttime activity... As a test I used only eight drops once before bed, and I could not get to sleep for several hours. And my rest was not deep!

As with all essential oils and all blends, you can take the exercise blend internally, if you are careful. Here we suggest using a drop in a teaspoon of honey. The oil takes effect in the digestive system and complements the defense blend. When used regularly, it will noticeably raise your energy level.

I have also seen the exercise blend help repair skin lesions. When the first sample of the exercise blend arrived in the US, a member of our team cut himself with a knife and applied it on the cut. The cut healed much faster than normal and was hardly noticeable within a few days.

Man's Intelligence Joined with Nature's Genius

The more I study the world of aromatic plants, the more I love them. Of the first five blends, the exercise blend is the richest in many ways. It has the largest number of essential oils (a total of eleven main ones) and its richness also stems from their variety and their harmonious synergistic effects. Even when diluted, it communicates a powerful synergy.

It was created using a different approach than with the defense blend. With the defense blend, I started with biochemical families, then selected the appropriate aromatic molecules and finally ended by choosing relevant essential oils. My goal with the defense blend was to respond to bacterial/fungal aggression. Thus it was logical to think in the medical and scientific way.

With the exercise blend, my goal and approach was totally different. The exercise blend is at the heart of wholeness. It embraces health rather than fights disease. Its purpose is not to ward off an attack. It is more like a military march to improve the morale and courage of your body's 'soldiers'—your muscles, joints, and overall energy.

The first aromatic plant I used is a very famous one—**Rosemary** *(Rosmarinus officinalis)*. You will not be surprised that I love this essential oil, because it is also the name of my wife Rose-Marie. Rosemary has several chemotypes according to the country in which it grows. For the exercise blend, my choice is the rosemary that grows in Tunisia in North Africa. I prefer low camphor content. Camphor is an aromatic molecule that belongs to the family of ketones. Though mild, it still belongs to a neurotoxic category inside the family of the ketones. It is for this safety reason that I chose the low camphor Rosemary from Tunisia.

You already know that, like ancient societies, we pay attention to the laws of the signatures or "signs of nature." When you look at rosemary, there are striking elements. The plant is almost a miniature tree. It grows fairly tall and has wood all along the plant. The leaves look more like the needles of conifers than broad leaves. Their pointed ends indicate strong and forceful energy. Because it contains a large percentage of cineole, this chemotype of rosemary combines symbolically the power of the eucalyptus with the power of the conifers. Tunisian rosemary brings a lot of energy into the muscles, the joints and the commanding nerves.

The 'energy' that I refer to here is not the Western concept of energy studied in physics, expressed in 'joules' or 'calories'. We think wholistically and we have to perceive the word 'energy' in the approach of oriental medicine. The Chinese call it 'Chi'. An increase of 'Chi' or subtle form of energy enables your muscles and also your entire body/mind unit to manifest strength and resistance.

The oil that accompanies and reinforces rosemary is **niaouli** *(Melaleuca quinquenervia viridiflora)*. Niaouli is easy to use for external application. It is also part of the respiratory blend. Yet, based on the traditional use in the islands where the tree grows, it makes sense that niaouli essential oil has wound-healing properties and can also be used for its deeper repairing action inside joints and muscles. We are not looking for a quick painkiller, but rather for restoring and mending inside living tissues.

Peppermint essential oil is a must here, as it was in two of my other blends. It is interesting that while the amount in the exercise blend is the same as in the defense blend, its role and its effect is changed by the presence of the other essential oils in the blend. It appears—and you may test this on yourself—that using the defense blend in the evening will not disturb your sleep. This is not true for the exercise blend. There is not enough peppermint in this blend to use it as an anesthetic or painkiller. There is quite enough, however, to use it as a tonic and mild stimulant, especially in synergy with rosemary and several other of the more "yang" essential oils.

Lavandin abrial and **geranium** (scented pelargonium) essential oils bring balance, so the strength of the exercise blend is somewhat moderated and kept under control.

Bay laurel *(Laurus nobilis)* essential oil distilled from the leaves gives the exercise blend interesting properties that do not just pertain to the physical level. It is true that bay laurel has had a long and traditional use in the management of rheumatism, in particular whenever there is a tendency toward sclerosis. But its presence inside the exercise blend can bolster self-confidence. This is important in any competitive activity even when you are only competing with yourself.

Clove bud, nutmeg, ginger and **black pepper** are classical essential oils used for warming the joints and muscles, and all are present in the exercise blend. These are well known for increasing energy and also for reducing pain. Their quantity is rather low so the blend keeps a final good balance.

A very small amount of genuine essential oil of **wintergreen** *(Gaultheria fragrantissima)* from Nepal gives the blend a final touch of pain-controlling action, but I kept it to a minimum because the primary function of this blend is to energize. It contains a natural methyl salicylate, which has a powerful scent of its own, but is subtle here, because of its low concentration.

I chose the Nepal wintergreen for its excellent quality, which is far better than common man-made methyl salicylate of most wintergreen flavorings.

The proportion of each ingredient plays a major role in the final blend. It is like cooking! An Indian curry may be very mild or extremely hot, according to the dosage of the spices. The same applies to blending essential oils. A blend intended for pain killing might include some of the same ingredients, but they would be mixed in very different proportion, completely changing the effect of the blend.

My "All Joints" Application

To understand the "all joints" technique, you must first understand its underlying principles. My goal is to put all my patients in charge of their own health. And I have learned that when they understand the reasons behind what I ask them to do, they will follow a regular health routine that will bring about lasting and truly effective results.

In treatments from many non-Westernized cultures, an image of the body and its various organs (with their reflex points) is represented on the soles of the feet as well as on the hands and on the ears. A less well known fact is that this projection of the whole body is made by some cultures, on each joint of each limb. You find it on the ankle, the knee, the hip, as well as on the wrist, the elbow, and the shoulder. This understanding is supported from a western neurological point of view.

From a Chinese medical perspective, the joints are said to be potential barriers to the flow of energy in the meridians. Or it might make more sense for us to think of the picture of a lock on river. Whenever a joint is massaged, it helps the flow of energy. Using essential oils increases greatly the effectiveness of simple hand massage, which is what I do on all the joints for this application.

Dilute the exercise blend in carrier oil and simply hand massage each joint for one or two minutes. If you want quicker penetration—within seconds—blend the oil with a light natural cream, or a lotion, the more natural the better. One reason for using the lotion-assisted dispersion of essential oils is that the molecules become ionized and the energy available to you immediately is much greater.

You may choose to mix five drops of exercise blend with a teaspoon of natural sea salt, stir well and dilute this aromatic salt in 200 ml of pure water in a large glass. Then, you 'dynamize' your aromatic water by turning clockwise with a chopstick for thirty seconds, until you see a lovely 'vortex' (spiral) being formed. This aromatic water is poured into a sprayer. You can then spray this aromatic saline solution on your joints and quickly massage them or briskly rub them with your fingers.

For a longer massage, use 10 ml of carrier oil to ten drops (more or less) of the exercise blend. We are not as concerned here with the exact quantity being used as we are with the quality of the oil. This is often challenging for my patients to understand. Think of it like this. When an obese person needs energy, he eats huge quantities of rich, processed foods and receives very little energy from it. A thin marathon runner controls his food carefully and shows an incredible energy capacity from far less food. His diet is many times less rich than the obese person, and yet he feels many times more energetic. If the quality of the food is high, a much lower quantity will deliver abundant energy.

Begin the 'all joints' application on the left ankle. Massage the aromatic oil all around it for one minute. Then do the same on the right ankle for one minute. Then massage the left knee—front, rear, and on the sides. Follow by massaging the right knee. Then massage the left hip and along the rim of the left iliac bone. Do the same on the right side.

Massage around each wrist, each elbow, and each shoulder, moving from left to right on each joint.

If you are using water or lotion for diluting the blend you may move more rapidly because of the faster absorption. After the oils have been absorbed, you will feel a definite increase of energy not only in your body but also in your psyche. You may also feel an interesting sensation in your *lungs,* your *nose*, and your entire *respiratory system.* All your systems are activated when you use the exercise blend. I repeat, don't do this massage before retiring. It's too energizing.

The "Whole Spine" Application

Another powerful external technique is a spinal massage you do on yourself. It is easier to demonstrate than to describe. You start at the tail bone or sacrum area and continue up the lower back or lumbar spine upward as far as you can, even if, in the highest area of the back, you need to use the back of your hand and fingers. You should be able to reach the area above where the kidneys are located. Then reach your hand over your shoulder and continue the application on the rest of the dorsal area or upper back. When you reach the base of the neck or cervical spine, massage it carefully, decreasing the pressure if it is sensitive.

Naturally, it is easier if a spouse, a friend, or one of your children can do this massage for you. You will feel a lot of energy from this massage throughout your body all day long. Others may even notice something lighter and more energetic about you.

When another person performs the massage along your spine, I suggest using clockwise movement on every part. Some books tell you to use clockwise movements for bringing Yang energy and counter-clockwise for Yin energy. I have a different opinion. I think it is possible to obtain a dispersion of energy (yin type of effect) by massaging clockwise but enlarging progressively the diameter of the circles in a kind of growing and extending spiral. It is also possible to concentrate the energy by turning clockwise and doing the massage from large circles to smaller ones.

You can also vary the speed of the movement. The Yin action is slower; the Yang action is faster.

In contrast to what many people would believe at first glance, the yin type of action is deeper and the yang type is more superficial. So, we can summarize it in this way:

a) Dispersion of energy (Yin action) = increasing circles in slow movements with a bit more of pressure.
b) Concentration of energy (Yang action) = decreasing the circles, with faster movements and a bit less of pressure.

It is true that the nature of the exercise blend is yang. Yet, in the way you choose to apply it, and by using a lower or higher concentration, you have the flexibility of bringing nuances in the primary action of the blend. But the orientation of the movement and the change in pressure and speed represent a far better way to disperse or concentrate energy than massaging counter-clockwise which is not very wise, especially on the trunk. Massaging the abdomen counter-clockwise is not consistent with the natural peristaltic flow of digestion—it pushes back the feces in the colon, which is potentially harmful.

A gentle clock-wise abdominal massage with the exercise blend diluted in carrier oil is excellent for those whose bowels do not function smoothly (for expelling the feces). However, if constipation is a result of spasms and blockages, it may be wiser to use a different blend—the calming blend discussed in the next chapter. But even the exercise blend, sufficiently diluted and properly applied clockwise in the yin style, can be effective here.

In case of yin constipation (a lazy colon), massage clockwise in narrower circles until you reach the navel area where you will work at a higher speed and not press too deeply.

It is good to accompany the external use of this blend with the internal intake of a drop. Avoid massaging the abdomen close to mealtime. It is safest if done one half hour before, or three hours after, a meal.

Special Note: Anyone who is prone to high blood pressure should not use the exercise blend frequently over a long period of time. There is a risk of increasing the blood pressure. Occasional use is not a problem. By using a full natural health program of sound nutrition, regular exercise, relaxation, and healthy thoughts, high blood pressure will often be relieved or at least under control.

Other Potentials

The exercise blend is excellent for massaging the feet, provided it is not done in the evening. It is especially good for those whose feet tend to always be cold due to poor capillary circulation.

The exercise blend can also help wounds to heal, especially in case of superficial cuts.

Because of its "hot" action, you may not want to use the exercise blend too often during the hottest days of the summer.

A possible nuance, that makes sense from the energy medicine point of view, is the case where you swim many hours each day, in lakes or in the sea or the ocean. Your presence in cold water for quite a long time will result in the accumulation of some 'cold energy' into your organism. Regularly using the exercise blend in this 'intense swimming context' is usually very beneficial.

Conversely, during cold weather the exercise blend is a wonderful stimulant. Eight of its essential oils come from subtropical or tropical countries where they have taken their energy from direct sun.

Individuals with what is known as the hippocratic nervous temperament will get the greatest benefit from using the exercise blend regularly, in particular during the colder and wetter seasons of the year. You will recognize these individuals because they are typically cold and dry. They tend to be more slender and seem to stay that way whatever they eat. They are very sensitive to the cold and to humidity, and they seem to catch the first bug that happens to be around (which is more likely to come from the inside, as you now know).

They are prone to ear, nose, and throat as well as respiratory infections, and possibly allergies (in particular after many courses of antibiotic treatments). Their level of immune defense is often quite low. They tend to like salty foods more than sweet ones, and you will often see them add salt to their food, even before tasting it. They are typically emotional, and depression is common. They are capable of becoming very enthusiastic, but it does not last long enough. They are often sensitive to music and many forms of artistic expression. Relationships play a major role in their psychological life. When they are in love, they are capable of anything. When they have no one to love them and for them to love, they are almost dead.

I am not saying that the exercise blend will totally transform them. But its regular use will definitely help correct the excesses in their temperament, and bring them a greater resistance to disease, and provide a better balance of disposition. You can see that the use of this essential oil blend goes well beyond the range of allopathic medicines! That is the beauty of the wholistic approach.

Other Uses of the Exercise Blend

If you are familiar with the nature of the essential oils in the exercise blend, you realize that rosemary, bay laurel, peppermint, clove buds, nutmeg, ginger, and black pepper are all used as herbs or spices in the kitchen, in cooking, and in seasoning. If mankind has used them in this way for thousands of years, it is for good reason! And all the work we do today to preserve healthy intestinal flora, is a striking confirmation of the intuition and the wisdom of our ancestors who had plants as their pharmacy, or you might say "farmacy."

The exercise blend can be used in food preparation just as you would use dried herbs or spices in your cooking. Naturally, because of the concentration of essential oils you must use minute amounts and must be sure that your essential oils are of the highest quality. In my mind, a low quality product has no place in your life, be it internally or externally absorbed.

For internal use, mix a trace of the oil into water with a toothpick or a chopstick and mix it vigorously to disperse it. You can also mix a drop in a small spoon of honey or fruit jam. It will activate your digestion and have some anti-infectious action. Dispersing a trace in a fruit juice is an easy and nice way of absorption. Whenever you disperse in a liquid, turn fifteen seconds clockwise before drinking it.

It is not just what enters your mouth, but what your body does with it, that really counts. Chewing correctly is the first mechanical step. The internal intake of a drop of the blend will exert a triple action—a definite antiseptic activity, a good activation of all the secretions in the digestive system, and a better movement of the smooth muscles, from the stomach to the rectum.

You may wonder about the properties of the cineole found in niaouli, rosemary, and bay laurel essential oils. You already know that the best way to tackle any respiratory problem involving thick mucous is to begin with improving the digestive system. The cineole molecules do stimulate and open the mucous membranes in the respiratory system, but they also stimulate the mucous producing glands inside the digestive system itself. This digestive system support, in turn, strengthens and supports the respiratory system. Again we see the multiple action effect of essential oils on the whole organism.

The absorption of a single drop, even in the evening, does not appear to disturb the sleep.

As you learn to use it properly, the exercise blend will become a great companion helping you to become strong, active, self confident, and trusting. As you use it, even in small amounts, you will feel results in all aspects of your life. Its warm action should be complemented by an opposite, cooler action, which will be the subject of our next chapter.

Chapter 17: The Calming Blend and the Intimacy Blend

Now it is time for a treat—two blends that everyone will find delightful. The first is the calming blend, and the second is the intimacy blend. Both of these blends are used for dealing with unhealthy stress that limits our full potential for wonderful health and great relationships.

Millions of pages have been written on the subject of stress. But, from all I have read from doctors and psychologists, no one appears to have the final answers. The aromatic way to deal with stress is completely different from the allopathic way.

They've Got It Wrong Once Again.
As a physician I respect the immense work that medical studies and clinical work represent. I went through it. But we have to face the fact that in the end, for patients all over the world the common answer is still drugs, drugs, and ever more drugs. For all types of stress, the medical establishment prescribes more and more psychoactive allopathic medications. Since eating is our most beloved activity, we must have our 'miracle happiness pills' to hide the truth and cheat ourselves out of true happiness and wonderful relationships.

Attention deficit hyperactive disorder has been diagnosed and misdiagnosed all over America. Everywhere children are bombarded with amphetamine-line drugs at a very young age. Recent news has documented that the medical establishment is even involved in the 'creation' of diseases so they can find a 'weapon' to cure them. Where is common sense and authentic health care at times like these?

Although the medical knowledge that comes out of the universities is becoming progressively more wholistic, the daily practice is far from what it should be. Doctors are all taught that antibiotics should no longer be prescribed as they have been for anything, everything, and nothing! But as long as there are no alternatives from the pharmaceutical establishment, the doctor does not know what to do. So he falls back into the same *pattern of easy answers from 'miracle pills.'*

Similarly your doctor knows that prescribing psychoactive drugs may make your brain become dependant on chemical 'crutches' and alter its harmonious functioning, but he does not know what else to do! Here again, *aromatic medicine has efficient answers to offer.*

However, if a patient is not willing to undertake any change in his lifestyle, and is only looking for a 'magic pill' to save him or her from having to make those changes, why would he or she ever consult a health professional that was prepared to spend a hour with him and offer what he truly needs? For most people five minutes with the doctor and a magic pill are, at this stage, the best the medical community can do.

There are many ways of dealing with stress apart from drugs. In fact, our "drug" responses include many other harmful chemical molecules such as tobacco, alcohol, caffeine, and a vast array of illegal, prescription, and over-the-counter drugs.

Stress in itself is not a disease. Stresses are like microorganisms, some come from the outside, and others come from the inside. The same situation can be experienced very differently by two people, just as the same bacteria may trigger a serious infection in one person and leave another totally unharmed. The best way to work on debilitating stress is from the inside.

Our 'aromatic way' always works best with patients who come to us *in the right frame of mind:* When a patient asks, "what can I learn to do to help myself and to help members of my family to feel better and more relaxed?" I know I can help them.

Stress As Seen From a Wholistic Perspective

Stress is merely tension accompanied with misdirected, uncontrolled, negative emotion. I focus on *the way the stressed person reacts,* not on the event that triggers the stress. The sprinter at the starting block waiting for the signal, has to be in a state of intense tension, physically and psychologically. But this tension is not a negative, misdirected, or controlled emotion. Some writers call positive stress *'eu-stress.'* 'Eu' is the Greek root for happy. The opposite could be called 'dis-stress.' The sprinter makes good use of stress.

It is difficult to achieve deep relaxation, once an intense condition of stress is over. The best way for a muscle to function is to be capable of intense contraction and then be able to become fully relaxed. In either a flaccid or a spastic state it becomes useless.

It is likewise healthy to express emotion intensely but in a controlled, positive way. This type of 'letting go' is healthy for our mental and physical condition. **Repressed negative emotions lie at the root of almost any disease expressed by the body.**

It is because essential oils are endowed with the double power of working on both the physical level and the mental level that they are absolutely unique and irreplaceable for dealing with stress.

The aromatic molecules that nature has invented for obtaining positive release in our body/mind unit are the ethers and above all the esters. In the make up of the calming blend, the esters play a primary role. In the intimacy blend, they play an important yet supportive role. Both blends complement each other and are logically grouped in the same chapter.

We all know that the olfactory organs have a direct link with the part of the brain where emotions are located. And there is also a strong relationship with memory. These ideas have been well supported with advanced studies on the relationships between the brain and the sense of smell.

I created these two blends with a keen awareness that they both had to create a beautiful aromatic 'memory.' They must 'whisper to your nose,' and at the same time create a wonderful sense of touch. They must communicate positive anticipation.

As I mentioned earlier, I have repeatedly observed a kind of a 'yawning reflex' to essential oil scents. By analyzing several features of my own yawning response, I can identify powerful effects of single oils and blends. Breathing the calming blend almost immediately triggers a yawning response that is very deep and satisfying, which is a good sign of its straightforward action.

The mind-healing process that olfaction may trigger is unbelievably powerful. Because the mind and the body are both involved, the patient must be *convinced of this power.* I am not saying that I want to create a placebo effect. But I do wish to avoid what is known as the 'nocebo' effect! This means that, even if a healing process is effective and real, *the mere fact that you do not believe in it, is enough to cancel its potentially positive effect, and sometimes even reverse it!* That is truly a mental barrier!

Swallowing an allopathic medication takes you two seconds. Getting involved in the olfactory whole-healing and transforming experience is altogether different. You need to have a pleasant atmosphere and be mentally prepared. It will not work in a noisy bar filled with smokers! It is reverent; it has to be done with a complete openness, deep gratitude, and sense of respect for these wonderfully complex aromatic molecules.

A session of music therapy or even a nice meal is the same. You need to be prepared to enjoy them. A truly satisfying intimate experience is not a one minute 'event' but rather an anticipated experience that must be prepared for mentally and emotionally in order to bring about a complete feeling of wholeness and deep relief of tensions. This feeling and this relief are by themselves powerful and profound healing factors.

I am impressed with the immediate and immense pleasure that comes from smelling these blends when you are in a receptive frame of mind. They are like the strains of long-forgotten music that restore powerful memories from the first time you heard them.

The Aromatic "Jewels" in the Calming Blend

Man's longing for beauty and creativity leads him to create artistic jewelry. Just as a queens crown calls for the most beautiful and precious jewels our selection of essential oils for these blends which are designed to effect the mind, must be done carefully.

The foundation oils of the calming blend are **true lavender** and **Lavendin abrial** of the highest organic quality. I next chose an essential oil extracted from the leaves of the bitter orange tree or **Petitgrain bigarade.** I have found it essential for helping patients to 'let go' of whatever emotional baggage they are carrying. It assists in all types of emotional 'forgiving' and releasing the negative emotions of the past. **Egyptian geranium** brings all its warmth to the heart and is a wonderful complement for lavender and *Petitgrain bigarade.*

The final ingredient is the exquisite **ylang ylang extra**--a supreme treat in the psycho-healing process. A few other essential oils finalize the more subtle aspects of the formula. Now contrast these ingredients with those of the intimacy blend.

Key Ingredients in the Intimacy Blend

With the intimacy blend, we are heading for paradise. If you recall what I told you in the chapter on lemon essence, you will remember that my choice for intimate expression can only be Sicilian organic **orange essence,** cold pressed from the peel.

When it is complemented by the **Egyptian geranium** essential oil and the delicious aroma of **ylang ylang extra,** you are experiencing aromatic delight. **Clary sage** adds a special edge and a few other essential oils all combine to make one's heart soar.

Now I want to explain several ways of working with the calming blend and the intimacy blend to make the most of their transforming power.

Using the Calming Blend

The calming blend, as you can guess from its name, is very yin just as the exercise blend is yang. According to the way you use it, the degree of dilution, the length of time you are exposed to its influence, the time of day you use it, and finally your own state of receptivity, the intensity of its yin influence can vary significantly. It is designed to be enjoyed on the skin, in the respiratory system, and in the digestive system.

Ideally a full session with the calming blend should be like a small vacation or calming retreat that you decide to give to your mind and your body. Choose a moment during which you know you will not be disturbed. Your session can take place in your bedroom or in any room chosen for relaxation. Make sure it is warm enough because you will fall in a state of such deep relaxation that having to get up for blanket would interrupt the relaxation.

Enjoy a trace of the calming blend with some honey or you can create an herbal tea with a small drop of the calming blend diluted in honey. This is the first step. Remember to drink it in a respectful way like you may have seen the Japanese do in their tea ceremony.

Then lie in your bed or wherever you choose to recline. Apply a drop of the blend on the heart chakra in the middle of the thorax and a drop on the nape of the neck. You may decide to apply a drop on the anterior fontanelle (where a baby's soft spot is located on the top of your head) if you wish.

You apply a trace on a blotting paper or tissue and keep it under the nose. Some patients have actually taped the blotting paper to their nose so that the air blown out of the nostrils does not remove it. Close your eyes and prepare for your calming journey. Later you may try to relax both with and without the blend. You will discover that the time it takes to go into a relaxed state is reduced manyfold when you are using the blend. Within seconds, the tensions of your mind/body unit taper off and drop, and your mental travel begins. Let me describe a possible session with the goal of internal purification and psycho-spiritual transformation. These would be words of instruction I would give to my patient or myself.

> *"Lie quietly on your back and breathe deeply from your abdomen. Hold the air in a few seconds, exhale deeply, and keep the lungs empty for a few seconds. You may feel tingling sensations in many parts of your body. Sense the energy of aromatic plants circu lating everywhere. Many hidden and unconscious blockages are set free and the way is opened for you to reconnect with your calmer self. This is a time to let go and leave behind the baggage of negative emotions you carry that creates such a stressful burden in your daily life. Only positive emotions have a place in your mind. You are filled with generosity and an immense sense of gratitude. As a unique human being, you have a consciousness of your value to others coming from your gifts and creativity in whatever field you work. You will now see things, people, and events with new eyes. Imagine yourself creating harmonious human relationships, here and now."*

This example of guided meditation is but one of many possible types of scripts you can go through to bring about deep relaxation.
What would become of your house if you never cleaned it? Your internal "house" requires at least the same attention, and probably much more. The teachings of all religions and spiritual disciplines recommend as hygiene for the soul, a daily mental exercise similar to this. Keeping your "internal house" clean is a lifestyle choice. If you do not *do it yourself,* there is no one on this planet who will do it for you.

Your encounter with essential oils may be a unique opportunity for you to take a new direction in your life for yourself, for your family, and for all the others around you. As you regularly create these aromatic experiences centered on the way you want to become and how you want to live your life, you will notice marked improvements in your internal life and health as well as in your external behavior. Others will feel it too. This aura of calm determination and the new peaceful yet strong way of tackling problems will improve all the most significant relationships in your life.

One of my deepest convictions is that aromatic plants crave to help mankind come to a new level of health, well being, and consciousness.

As you read these paragraphs you may think such an emotional transformation is not possible. You may feel it is too good to be true or that I am going too far. But you can at least admit that offering a judgement without any personal first-hand experience is tantamount to offering a judgement on Bach's music without ever having heard a single composition of Bach!

My advice is simply to do it under the appropriate conditions I describe and with a receptive state of mind. The minimum that you will feel is a profound relaxation. You may even fall asleep. The internal healing will occur even during the sleep. When you wake up you will be in a different state of mind.

This is completely different from the action of allopathic drugs. It is also light years away from the effects of illegal drugs.

From Drugs to Aromatics—From Death to Life

It is common for uninformed persons to think that essential oils are a new kind of drug. We know that the chemical structure of drugs is very specific. They enter into the brain and act on receptors that will, for a while, put the user into an 'artificial paradise.'

Think of the aromatic molecules resonating with the receiving cells of the body (especially the olfactory cells). It is an action of vibration. It is like a great composer's music coming in contact with your eardrum. It vibrates and creates pleasure.

There is a basic question I like to ask those who tell me that essential oils are 'just another drug.' The question is, How do you feel after the experience? In the case of drugs, real ones, there is a definite state of depression and feeling low, which inevitably forces the drug user to addiction, dependancy, and abuse. There is no way that essential oils could trigger the same morally destructive effects!

When I decide to give to myself an 'aromatic spiritual retreat,' it is never one of uncontrollable compulsion! It is always a *free choice*, as it would be to pray, to sing, to paint, to write, to dance, to meditate, or to perform any other kind of *creative activity.* When the aromatic journey is over, there is a feeling of wholeness, of peaceful well being, and of being in harmony with the world. And this feeling is a *lasting one.* You do not feel like doing the experience half an hour later, like the smoker who finishes one cigarette and is compelled to light the next one. Drugs bring no *authentic satisfaction*. On the contrary, it is their nature to leave you in this enslaved state.

With aromatic plants and essential oils, your body is relaxed, your heart is joyful, your mind is clear, your soul is purified and your spirit reaches a lofty position. Who could ask for more?

The Calming Blend in its Simpler Applications

Your calming blend has strong antispasmodic properties. Dilute it in a carrier oil and massage the areas that will benefit from its relaxing action. Use an average of five drops for a tablespoon of oil. It can be between three and eight drops. Most people prefer a massage on the nape of the neck and the trapezius muscles. If you are alone, you can give yourself this massage.

If you do it on yourself, sit with a cup with the mixture within reach. Dip your fingers in the oil and begin by gently apply the oil along the muscles of the neck. You simply turn in a clockwise direction over the whole area. Then put your elbows on the table and bend your head forward and you massage in a downward direction, starting from the occipital bones of the head and massaging with an increasing yet moderate pressure down to the trapezius muscles. This massage is easy to perform, and within one or two minutes, the effect is a profoundly relaxing one.

The neck is a crucial area for creating relaxation because it connects the head and the trunk. This massage is most important for all those who spend eight hours a day in front of their computer.
In addition to the neck, any muscle that feels tense or contracted can benefit from a massage with the diluted calming blend. Whenever it is possible, you should ask your partner to give you a full massage along the spine, from neck to sacrum. *I do not advise driving at night (or even during the day for receptive persons) after such a massage.*

Children who are hyperactive and cannot sustain their attention need to be approached wholistically, starting with healthy nutrition. A diluted massage in the evening or before going to bed will help to decrease their hyperactivity.

For those who are prone to high blood pressure, the calming blend can help with the nervous side of their problem.

If you wish to give a foot massage in the evening, it is better to choose the calming blend than the exercise blend! And conversely, do not use the calming blend before you have to be very active or before driving your car. It's just common sense.

The abdominal massage with the diluted calming blend is a good way to set free the blocked areas in the abdomen. You can perform the massage on five distinct levels: above the pubis, on the 'Hara' (four finger widths under the navel), around the navel, three finger widths above the navel and right under the sternum.

The other classical way is to start around the navel and increase the size of the clockwise circles until you follow the whole pathway of the colon. In that case, you may remember that you combine the right yin blend with the right movement: progressively larger circles, slowing speed and increased pressure. You may find several sensitive and blocked spots or areas. With a gentle and progressive work, you will be able to release the tensions. I prefer *to do these massages on myself rather than* to have someone else do it onto me (unless the person is a trained therapist). Someone else must massage my back if it is to be done properly, but I learn a lot when I analyze the possible tensions in my own abdominal area.

When you decide to perform the abdominal relaxation and massage on yourself, be aware that it is not something to do hastily or superficially. You have to take time in order to tame your tummy and make it a good friend. Believe me, this aromatic time that you spend represents an investment that will bring you a high return, not only in the better functioning of your digestive organs, but also *better control on your emotional reactions.* Ideally, this can be complemented by a work on the reflex points of the feet and possibly the ears (which will be demonstrated in lectures and workshops).

I warned you against using the calming blend before intense focused activity such as athletic competition. However, if you feel excessively nervous and tense, it is possible to use it in a more superficial way. This will work even better if you have been in the habit of practicing the deep relaxation I described. Your mind will be conditioned to react in a relaxed way when you breathe the calming blend. This means that a few sniffs will enable you to get rid of the useless or harmful tensions such as those that impede or decrease your ability to speak to a large crowd or perform in a critical event.

For those who have difficulty falling asleep, the calming blend should be massaged on the sides and nape of the neck, on the solar plexus, on the wrists (diluted) and an undiluted drop on the anterior fontanelle at bedtime. If you take sleeping pills and choose to reeducate your mind toward natural sleep, you will want to progressively decrease the dosage of the pills and use the calming blend on a regular basis. If you are not too strongly addicted, you will be able to stop using them within a month or two. Do not stop taking such allopathic drug overnight! Essential oils are not miracle medicines.

You will discover on your own many other uses for your calming blend, always in the areas of calming, antispasmodic, and, to some degree, anti-inflammatory uses. In case of inflammation, I often prefer mixing a few drops of the calming blend in a few tablespoons cold water to be applied with a gauze compress, cling film, and a bandage.

New Light Shed by Science, Medicine, and Psychology

You may have heard of all the stress research done to identify those with type A personalities who are more prone to physical damage due to stress. More recently that research has taken a turn toward attempting to identify the effects of living the spiritual teachings of service, unselfishness, peace, humility, self-mastery, and meekness.

A most interesting study was conducted by a team of cardiologists who examined by cardiac catheterization the coronary arteries of many patients. They confirmed that, "intermittent outbursts of heart activity from surges of hostility finally damage the heart. The surges of catecholamines and other brain hormones that occur during anger may contribute directly to both arterial injury and the deposition of plaque on arterial walls. Over time, repeated traumatic emotional reactions may also fray heart tissue fibers, which, in turn, may lead to the disorganization of the cardiac circuitry." (*The Healing Brain*, by Robert Ornstein, PhD and David Sobel, MD, Simon & Schuster, 1988)

Think now of the intense and ceaseless activity of Mother Teresa in India, in extremely difficult conditions. Think of the age she reached before her heart said 'too much is too much.' I am certain that, had she been a business woman, mainly working for her own profit and not for the common good, her heart would have failed much earlier in her life, even with a far less intense activity!

Here is what is said in the Ornstein & Sobel book, "Scherwitz and colleagues speculate that it is not the activity of people that is dangerous to the heart, nor the hurry or the speed, but the selfishness that underlies it. They assert that if individuals are ambitious, competitive, or time urgent for purely selfish reasons, they may be at greater risk than if they are ambitious or competitive to serve others or higher ideals. In our terms, the latter are those who are interested in maintaining a stable connection with the larger organism of humanity as a whole. This perspective would also explain why those people who can look outward at others, at a pet, at a plant, might be responding to a deeper need within our brains than we and they know about." (Op. cit.)

Through my years as a medical doctor, I have come to realize that purely selfish intentions would kill the essence of my work with patients and would result in very limited and poor results. This in turn would lead to a great deal of stress within me as well as my patients.

The Meaning and the Use of the Intimacy Blend

As a physician I feel fortunate to be able to take the necessary time to spend with my patients so that their lives may take a new direction toward wholeness. For you to better understand what I mean by that, let me report the following clinical case.

> A woman in her thirties, a mother of two young children, came to me with a diagnosis of multiple sclerosis. Her husband accompanie her. She had typical symptoms such as sensitivity in her lower left leg. The neurologist had given the diagnosis after an MNR examination of her brain and analysis of her spinal fluid. The only answer he offered was to wait until a new crisis occurred, and then he would provide her with the usual allopathic treatments which in realitytreat nothing in depth apart from suppressing the external manifestations.
>
> Before I accept patients, I make sure they have the right attitudes toward healing. I will spend as many as two to four hours with them. They usually travel from far away and have to be prepared to follow a healing pathway that has nothing in common with swallowing the latest allopathic miracle pill!
>
> It is important that both the husband and wife are ready for a big change in their lives. This woman was a doctor of computer science and her husband owned a health food shop. They were perfectly aware of the efforts they would have to make, and they had accepted all the prerequisite conditions.

I will not analyze here her full clinical history. But when I asked her, as any MD or wholistic health professional should do, about her sexual life, she told me, or rather her husband told me that their sexual life was almost non-existent. When I asked her whether other doctors had asked her about this subject, she told me that no one had. To her it was as if the part of her body that was under the navel had strictly no right to exist! When time had come for her to give birth to her two children, the uterus had no capacity of contraction, and she was obliged to undergo a cesarean section each time.

What was even more striking in her case was the fact that when she was younger, she had nosebleeds all the time (there is a connection between the nose and sexual life). One day the bleeding was so abundant, that she had to go to the hospital.

The doctor told her to refrain from sneezing and blowing her nose for a few hours, so the bleeding would not reoccur. In fact, she totally blocked her nasal passages for days; the mucous accumulated and reached the sinuses. That single event was the beginning of a block age that extended to her female cycle.

What I want you to understand is that there was a logical development in her story, but no one cared to inquire? And even if the specialist had asked those questions, to him it would have meant nothing since he does not have the key for interpreting these different stages of the disease. You know that the pituitary gland is closely related to the nose and the sinuses. Inflammation in the nose and sinus area always has serious consequences for the functioning of the pituitary. This malfunction, even in a subtle and hidden way, plays a role in autoimmune diseases, and more specifically multiple sclerosis. Now, it all began to make sense to me...

My patient received a full education about what she and her husband would have to do at home. Foot reflexology, massage of the spine, local applications and internal intake of essential oils, all were integrated into her life. In addition the couple was asked to give each other a massage with the diluted intimacy blend. It was not in the sense of moving toward a sexual act right away, but much more for what I call sensual re-education—simply learning the pleasure of touching and feeling in a healthy sexual way.

The whole program was applied with great care. After the first three months, great changes occurred. All neurological manifestations dis appeared (but in MS, this is common). More telling was the complete change in their life together. They now have a normal sexual life, and, from a psychological angle, she feels like a new woman. And she is. Incidentally, she has found a very strong religious connection, and her husband, who was rather distant (but not closed) on this subject, now follows in a dedicated way, the same spiritual direction.

As I said to her, 'If you had not had your disease, you would never have consulted me. Your blockages would have created sooner or later another kind of disease, perhaps even more serious. And your relationship with your husband would have been seriously endangered. Thus, you can be grateful for your disease because it helped you live again through a real rebirth, with your husband, in the spiritual sense.'

Let me ask you, "Do you think it would have made sense just to hand out a vial of the intimacy blend and think that all their problems would be fixed as if by magic? Our intimacy blend should never be perceived as a type of "natural Viagra!" We have too much respect for love, human sexuality, and intimacy in general to reduce its physical manifestation to a local congestion. Concerning sexuality, as in all other fields, our attitude is a wholistic one. All that you do in a healthy life style is the best possible preparation for a happy sexual life.

When you use the first three more physically oriented blends—the respiratory blend, the defense blend, and the exercise blend—on a regular basis, you will activate most of your energy centers. Also, using the exercise blend, with essential oils from several hot spices, is a good way to activate the energy center connected with sexuality.

The place and the role of the intimacy blend is different from the calming blend. The intimacy blend is designed to be used in a diluted massage.

If a couple has a happy sexual life, it is lovely to accompany the foreplay period with a massage. Five to ten drops in a tablespoon of carrier oil will make a beautiful massage oil that both partners will enjoy.
For couples who occasionally have sexual difficulties, I recommend *the intimacy blend. But it is most important to use it first when all is going well.* Why? Simply because the sweet smell of the intimacy blend will be remembered. Its fragrance will become associated in the subconscious as well as the conscious mind with wonderful sexual memories. Then, when a time comes that it is more difficult to trigger a desire, the diluted intimacy blend can be used for a massage, and the desire and sexual energy will return more easily.

This memory connection may be used in other circumstances as well. You can choose to associate the intimacy blend with some of the most pleasant experiences of your life and, whenever you feel a bit low or somehow depressed or unwilling to do the good things you would like to do, inhaling the intimacy blend and applying a drop will help trigger the positive response that is linked with positive events.

Here again, you are using an aroma with your imagination to reinforce in your brain circuits things you want to remember. For example, inhaling the intimacy blend and applying one drop on the heart chakra could mean for you, after a few repetitions, a feeling of confidence and peace. Instead of using the heart chakra, you can choose to use two acupuncture meridians—the heart and the pericardium/sexuality medians located on the anterior part of the wrist—on the fold that is formed when you bend the hand, at the intersection of the center of the wrist and the line extending out from the little finger.

Apply a small drop on one wrist and gently turn this scented wrist onto the other one. When you use the intimacy blend on your wrists, you will enjoy it more because you so frequently bring your hands to your face and accidentally smell the aroma. As you enjoy the blend, think of personal affirmations such as the following:

> *I have the right and the will to feel happy and to make others feel happy. I have the right and the duty to be proud of my behavior and my transformation. I will follow the way to happiness and fulfillment respecting my choice of natural health and dedication to goodness, truth, beauty, and harmony. This aroma is there to remind me that life is generous with us when we respect and serve the Creator of life.*

Use your imagination to create a new and better reality for yourself. To some of you, this exercise may seem childish at first, but this is the way our brain functions! Why not use this olfaction/memory experience to overcome self-defeating behavior and create new ones. It is definitely less childish than rushing to the fridge when you feel unhappy.

In cases where real sexual problems exist, here are a few suggestions. A couple who is fundamentally in disagreement or opposition will find that using the intimacy blend cannot perform miracles. In such cases, the first step may be psychological or marriage counseling. If only one receives counseling, it will not give whole results.

It is true, that a happy sexual life can help to build a strong relationship, but if there no unity or kindness to add to the happy sexual life, the sexuality alone will not be sufficient to make the relationship a lasting one.

Conversely, when both partners are united in all other aspects, and when it is only the sexual aspect that is dysfunctional, there is no need to separate or divorce without attempting to improve the sexual aspect of your life. In such cases, you may need to consult a specialist. The use of the intimacy blend can play a complementary role, especially in the form of reeducation the senses.

In cases of premature ejaculation, sexologists have developed specific techniques for reeducating the male partner. A whole health program will contribute greatly to improving the situation. Both the calming blend and the exercise blend will bring their support in the reeducation process. Practicing deep breathing exercises with times of retention will definitely help with sexual control.

Other Applications of the Intimacy Blend

First a caution: the intimacy blend contains orange essence (not essential oil). As with all cold pressed citrus essences, you know that there is a risk of photosensitization in case of direct exposure to the sun within the twelve hours following the application on the skin. This is totally true for a neat application. For a diluted one, the risk is, of course, decreased. As with all the other blends, there is no problem in taking one or two drops internally.

Keep in mind that we do not use any kind of chemical fragrance in the blend. The high quality essential oils used in the blends and total absence of any solvents sets them apart from most of the products that you find everywhere under the name of aromatherapy or perfume.

Even though the essential oils of scented pelargonium (geranium), ylang ylang, and clary sage do not taste very good on their own, the fact that they are blended with the organic orange essence makes the taste quite acceptable.

Children enjoy the fragrance of the intimacy blend. Intimacy, as I use it here, does not limit itself to the intimacy of sexual contact. Some of the deepest forms of intimacy are expressed in sharing genuine love and commitment within the close family circle. The clasping of hands and the tender touching of a parent and child are deeply intimate experiences. Such an expression not only does not need any sexual involvement to convey love and caring, but the message of true intimacy and trust would be destroyed by sexual involvement.

Always dilute the intimacy blend when using it for a child's massage. Alternate it with the calming blend. These two blends are wonderful for calming hyperactivity. The intimacy blend is conceived as a treat you give to yourself and to others to convey love, tenderness, and caring. Certainly, all families need more tender, trusting, touching experiences to arm them against a most stressful and often prickly world where touching in a trusting way is almost impossible. You can imagine the emotional healing and strengthening of relationships that can take place between parents and children who feel comfortable giving calming massages to each other.
You can massage the feet, the legs, the back, the neck, and the arms. Avoid using the blend on the face.

The Intimacy Blend and Sleep
When you receive or give an intimacy blend massage before bed, you should expect to wake up in the morning well rested after a deeply quiet night. There are often many dreams. This dream- inducing or dream-enhancing action is fascinating.

When allopathic sleeping pills are used, their molecules often have a deleterious influence on what is called 'paradoxical sleep,' which relates to the occurrence of dreams. The act of dreaming is probably as vital to the health of the nervous system as the act of sleeping. When rats were deprived of the possibility of dreaming (they were monitored and awakened whenever the paradoxical sleep occurred), they became psychologically disturbed and preferred to die rather than not dream! When you embrace the aromatic way, you can enhance the quality of your nights in both kinds of sleep.

In the morning you feel that life is beautiful and you have a deep feeling of serenity in your mind. This is not to say that you are disconnected from the real world! Quite the opposite. You feel deeply connected to the world you live in and prepared to give the best of yourself.

Sexuality in Our Path to Wholeness—Finding Our Way Back

The meaning of healthy sexuality in its deepest sense is far above what I would call merely having sex. As men and women, we come together in a complementary harmony. In the modern world of successive separations and repeated divorces, the creation of this sacred union seems more a dream than a reality. It may be good business for lawyers, but, from a human and spiritual perspective, separation and divorce is such a waste and takes a terrible toll! If the sex act alone were able to resolve all the problems between a couple, it would be just too easy. One of the greatest problems of our day comes from the *separation between the sex act and true, intimate, and lasting love.*

In extreme cases, like in rape, the sex act may be followed by the murder of the victim. Where is love in such action? The sex of pediphiles involves intense suffering inflicted on the innocent. Where is love? There are many opportunities to express hatred, selfishness, and cruelty in lust and sex.

The way back to wholeness comes by reconnecting love and sexuality. As a doctor who takes the necessary time to hear many confessions, I am perfectly aware that it is important for both partners to have the sexual fulfillment that plays such an important role in healthy intimacy. An unsatisfactory sexual life creates blockages in the flow of energy inside the body, which can, in its turn, contribute to many different pathological manifestations both physical and psychological. And this is just as true for men as it is for women. Even a 100 % satisfactory sexual relationship is not sufficient for keeping the relationship alive. There must be true, unselfish, compassionate love. This is a principle that we cannot escape no matter how hard we try.

A self-centered obsession with the acts of sex is just another way of being destructively addicted and morally powerless, which is very similar to dependency on a drug. If you happen to be in such a terrible situation, a complete detoxification program is mandatory. There is no magic sex patch to stick on to the skin!

Following a healthy, active, and productive life is important for a healthy and fulfilling sexual life. In severe cases of sexual addiction specific counseling becomes indispensable. Here again, essential oils are not miracle cures to solve our most severe problems but simply tools to help us reconnect in a healthy way.

Using the intimacy blend with someone you love and are committed to helps you reconnect in an unselfish and loving way. This is far from self-indulgent slavery of sexual addictions. Sexual addictions lead to increasingly bizarre efforts to feel pleasure and away from wholeness.

By way of conclusion, I wish to refer to the symbol of the apple, the forbidden fruit. Let me ask you this question, How do you normally cut an apple, when you want to share the other half with someone you love? Naturally you cut it in the long or vertical way. And have you ever noticed the shape that is made when you cut an apple in this way. You will see the shape of the heart. This is a beautiful symbol that indicates to me *the way back to paradise.*

If you separate sex from love, you create obsession and slavery. If you choose the way of the heart, you and your companion will find your way back to paradise. The apple symbol expresses clearly that *there is only one way back to paradise, the way of love.*

Chapter 18 : My Practical Aromatic Experience

By Rose-Marie Pénoël

I am very pleased to complement my husband's writing with "a woman's input." I want to share with you the joy I feel in taking part in the natural health "awakening" taking place on the North American Continent. This project would not have been possible, had we not encountered partners with the capacity to understand the magnitude and meaning of the mission that beckons to all of us.

I wish to thank personally and deeply Ron Williams and his whole team for their dedication to the success of this worldwide project. Very special thanks go to Bill Fifield who worked so hard so that this book could be made available to you.

I would like to share with you a few ideas for helping the harmonious growth and supporting the steady extension of natural and aromatic practice on a family level. Our first book, *Natural Home Health Care Using Essential Oils* describes beneficial therapies and worthwhile instructions for dealing with specific home applications. I highly recommend it. This book, *Life Helping Life*, continues on with more detailed information regarding eight of the most basic single oils and five of the most useful blends. Daniel has already given you several comparisons to help you understand why we need both for integral aromatic practice. And it is very important for you to keep his explanations in mind.

Let's imagine the following scenario: a friend introduced you to essential oils or maybe you attended a lecture. And in the "heat of the moment", you decide to acquire all the essential oils and all the blends. Of course, you have also acquired the two books. Do you know what is likely to happen, once you come back home? You realize that you don't really know what to do with so many products in front of you! Your husband comes home and discovers those fragrant little vials. Do you dare tell him how much you invested? He asks you what you intend to do with them and you find yourself a bit embarrassed to give satisfactory and detailed answers. He is more likely to "smell a rat" instead of pleasant essential oils! He might think you were taken in by excited people who pushed you to purchase too much too soon. And, he might become cross with you. To avoid contention and becoming overwhelmed, I have a logical and systematic program for beginning your aromatic adventure. There are very good reasons for starting with a group of essential oils instead of just one or two vials. And in the beginning, everyone needs a guidebook to get started. You can be confident about what you're doing, and you are on the right track.

My Suggestions

My very first piece of advice is to read the book and make your personal notes while reading it. Even if practical brochures are made available, your own work and your reflection remain irreplaceable! There is something exciting and rejuvenating in being a student!

Second, start with a single oil. Learn about it. Use it. Experiment with it. When you are comfortable with its many applications, then go on to the next one. As you do this with the eight basic single oils you will begin to see and feel how essential oils can enrich and heal. I recommend starting with peppermint, then tea tree, then eucalyptus oil. Continue on with lavender and tropical basil. Finish the basic eight with Balsam fir, geranium and lemon. Next, select the blends you need and learn about them in the same way, one at a time. Use them on yourself. Do the little tests Daniel gives you. As you do this, you will develop the knowledge and experience and confidence in using essential oils to bless your life and the lives of your family.

The easiest way for you to start on the right track is to attend to a live seminar, either directly with both of us, or through someone who has received our training first hand. This kind of transmission from one level to the other, with practical demonstrations, is the best way for us to progress collectively. Acquiring skills in essential oil therapy is nothing like 'recreational fragrancing.' It is much more complex than buying a few bottles of sweet smelling oil! The apprenticeship is best transmitted from person to person, or from one trained person to a group.

Above all, pay serious attention to the chapter about safety. If you have young children, I remind you to *keep all essential oils out of their reach and to tightly close the caps.* I do love their nice presentation with the separate glass pipettes. This represents a great advantage for following the whole method with accuracy. However, this choice results in there being no childproof safety caps and no permanent stopper inserts, so we have to be doubly careful around children. Always keep a good carrier or vegetable oil on hand to dilute the oil if there are any adverse reactions. This is particularly important when using the blends. Because the synergy makes them more potent than single oils, blends should be diluted when applied. Also, when applying oils use the little finger rather than the index finger. This will lessen the possibility of accidentally getting essential oil's in the eye. Because it is important to be able to apply essential oils at the first sign a symptom is felt, it is wise to create a small pouch containing small bottles of oils to carry with you at all times.

Keep in mind that this program has to be *accompanied by some basic changes in your nutrition, or else your results will be impaired or diminished.* It is important to observe your own evolution, your reactions, your transformation, your new feelings, objectively over a period of several weeks. If you can take some basic notes, it's a good way to compare results and document your first steps on your aromatic pathway.

Spreading the Good News

Because you love helping others, after experiencing the wonderful results you get in working on so many common problems, you will find it very natural to talk with your friends. Be careful you do not behave in a 'pushy way'! First, check whether they do have some interest in natural health and in becoming responsible for it to a large extent. Some people are simply oriented toward an 'allopathic pill' approach and there is no way they would be excited about the possibilities of essential oils, or change their life, or change their way of thinking. Insisting or pressing further would trigger opposition from them. At least, they are aware that you have some interest in natural and aromatic care. If they want to know more, they can always come and ask you later.

The best way to create interest among your friends is to organize what I call 'an aromatic and natural health party'. In France, when I do this with Daniel, it takes place on Saturday afternoon, from 2 p.m. to 6 p.m. and we call it *'Initiation à la pratique aromatique familiale'* (initiation into family aromatic practice). It is important to have some nice incentive. A treat at the end of healthy recipes prepared with essential oils can be included. We have fun tasting them.

You can only organize such an event after you have gained enough confidence in your basic knowledge and practice with the oils. You must cover safety measures thoroughly. Explain the 'spirit' behind the use of essential oils vs. allopathic treatments and the possibilities that exist for caring for your family. The point is not for them to play 'the little doctor', but to increase progressively their capacity to manage their own health and the health of their family members.

Keep this picture in mind. You do not rush to the emergency ward of the hospital if you have a thorn in your finger. First, you take it away with fine tweezers and apply some disinfectant. It's very simple, yet not doing it may end up in with your emergency trip to the hospital a few days later.

Whatever you teach should be understood as common sense measures. It is better to prevent than to cure. And, in case of any problem, learning to perform immediately the right measures may prove health promoting, complication preventing and maybe even life saving. You should go through summary explanations about each essential oil in a logical order, in the order they are presented in the book. It is important to accompany each explanation with practical experiments. These can include the trace of tea tree on the tongue, the different ways of applying *Eucalyptus radiata,* what to do with peppermint and how to do it, how and when to use diluted essential oils, what is an aromatic compress and why it is better in some cases, etc. You get all this in the book and naturally, at the end of the party, your friends should have a book to take with them to read quietly in their home.

As it was your case at the very beginning, let them start with the essential oils that seem to suit them best, simply guiding them if they hesitate. You may present the blends briefly, but it is wiser to decide to organize a separate party later on for the blends. The last hour is spent on healthy nutrition. Making some aromatic recipes helps them understand that health and pleasure are quite compatible. Prepare some aromatic teas with essential oils in honey, using peppermint, tropical basil, and lemon. Use a drop blended in a fruit juice. Traces or minute amounts of lavender or even geranium may be interesting in special recipes! A drop of balsam fir, eucalyptus radiata or tea tree is quite tolerable. You will be amazed at your friends' reactions to these teas!

These are some basic guidelines for a successful and healthy party that can be reproduced at regular intervals. My greatest pleasure is to see that our contribution makes a significant difference in your life and in the overall health of your family.

You Can Feel Whole Again

If you asked me how I recognize that something is good, I answer. It makes me feel 'whole'. How do I feel whole? I feel my center. I feel my connection with the world 'above me'. I feel my connection with mankind and all living beings on this planet—humans, animals, plants. Even stones are taking part in the great cycles of the Biosphere.

I feel my connection with all those who worked so hard before us, all those who are working now and all those who will take over our mission when time comes for us to leave this planet. My life is purposeful and meaningful. My body, my heart, my mind, my soul and my spirit are one, united and integrated so I can live life with all the gifts and the wonders we receive each day.

I express my feeling of wholeness in all aspects of my life, especially the acts of movement and singing, which in its turn make me feel even more whole. And I encourage all of you to reconnect with your body, with your voice and with music.

Daniel has many things to share with you. I can say I have much to share also, but on a more subtle level. With the two of us accompanying you on your travel toward wholeness and whole life, you're about to attract all the positive energies and all the good influences you deserve. It does not mean that everything will be solved as if by magic! I simply mean that the way you perceive events and people around you, the way you perceive yourself and your own mission, will renew your vision of life on earth. From this wholistic perception, wholistic actions will result with positive effects.

Essential oils will definitely help you on this path of wholeness. We come to you with highly efficient practical tools and proven methods to help you and your beloved ones. We do it with our long years of experience and with our full dedication and entire sincerity. Our partners are filled with the same warm energy.

It is only by working together that we can make things change and the world evolve for the better. This is the love and soul that helps us live 'on earth as in Heaven'. This is the grace I wish for each of you and for all of us in this new era.

Rose-Marie Pénoël
Vallée de la Drôme
April 5, 2000.

CONCLUSION

Did you enjoy your aromatic journey? For me, it was also a growing experience. It made me re-discover, understand and endeavor to express more clearly much about essential oils in relationship to a program of whole life. I find myself once more 'born again' because of this exercise. Rose-Marie and I do hope you feel the same way

.

We are made in such a way that we do our best work for others. If you were having your dinner alone at home, would you organize a lovely presentation and a fancy meal? Would you put on your best clothes and have your hair done? Probably not.

Here, the desire to help you understand the wonders of the aromatic world put me back onto a track of intense effort, both in communicating better the things I take for granted and also in creating new essential oil blends for the kit. This would not have been possible without your interest and our common will to progress together.

The publishing of this first basic handbook coincides with our US arrival in April 2000 for a series of lectures. I am very grateful to Bill Fifield and to the network of friends who have worked 'day and night' to finalize the work within the printer's deadline.

It is important for you to read it, re-read it and absorb it. Additional complementary writings will follow to extend your knowledge and practice. Whenever possible, come and attend one of our live seminars; it is an experience for which there is no substitute.

When I say 'absorb it', I mean not only the data and techniques. I refer also to the spirit that pervades the entire writing, the spirit that teaches:

1. You are in charge of your own life and your own health.
2. Your choice of wholeness is indeed the right choice.
3. It is not just what you do, but how you do it and your motives that count most.
4. The way you choose will bear its fruit only after perseverance and steadiness.

5. Do not change everything at once in your life. If there is one thing to change first and above all the rest, it is your mental attitude toward life itself.
6. Do not impose anything on others. Be first an example of your choice for whole life.
7. Your motivation should be summarized by the motto: 'help, serve and network.'
8. Find the vertical connection in your life. It is the only way to endow it with full meaning and stable purpose.
9. Be prepared for profound changes.
10. There must be no attitude of competition in your mind. Consider all who work with essential oils your partners and your friends, even if they do not look at you this way. There is nothing more powerful than love in the entire Universe.
11. Nature is complex so we don't have to be.
12. Life helps life.

The integral aromatic way Rose-Marie and I teach is but one among many. It is our way and we are delighted to share it with you. We know it can help millions of individuals and families around the world.

Remember that the mission of aromatic plants and essential oils is to help us on all levels. If you begin using essential oils with gratitude, dedication and a sincere desire to work for the common good, your reward will be a strong body, a clear and open mind, a loving and generous heart, a pure soul and a lofty spirit.

Miracles are simpler than we think. Consider the miracle of breathing, the miracle of smiling, the miracle of walking, running, dancing, singing. And you will be able to say, "I love life!"

Dr Daniel Pénoël & Rose-Marie Pénoël
Vallée de la Drôme
April 15, 2000.